GOD
TOLD ME TO
TELL YOU!

GOD TOLD ME TO TELL YOU!

*An Expose On "The Word Of Knowledge"
As It Is Being Misused Today!*

Robert Lee Whitworth

New Leaf Press

P.O. BOX 311, GREEN FOREST, AR 72638

First Edition
1988

Cover Art: Bonnie Curnock

Typesetting: A.G.A.P.E. Graphics and Printing
Berryville, Arkansas 72616

Library of Congress Catalog Number: 88-62048

ISBN: 0-89221-159-8

TABLE OF CONTENTS

DEDICATION

To my precious wife Nona

for her months of patience

and prayers

while I wrote this book.

PREFACE

God did not tell me to write this book!

After thirty-four years of pastoring, I am now in my twenty-ninth year at the same church. I am urged to write because of the people who are mishandled by men in the charismatic pentecostal movement. The verse in I Corinthians 12:8 has been twisted and distorted to damage believers with their false "God told me to tell you." For years I have spoken out against what I know is wrong. The error perpetrated upon the millions on television, in prayer groups, and in church is exposed in this volume.

I have endeavored to explain the difference between TRUTH and ERROR in respect to the word of knowledge. Perhaps there are dangers in simplification and reduction, but as these pages unfold, one will see the purpose of this book.

To find order in a world of so many ism's, cults, and doctrines, one must rightly divide the written Word of God.

God is not the author of confusion. Every answer for man is in the written Word of God...the only TRUTH.

1

THE WRITTEN WORD
OF GOD

Soon after the "fall" of Jim Bakker, Oral Roberts made public the following prophecy for all to know and hear:

"...The Word of the Lord is in my mouth I say to you, dear brother, who is sowing discord among the brethren because you think that you are "holier than thou." Somehow Satan has put something in your heart that you're better than anybody else, you have gone and have gotten in touch with the people in headquarters who are holding on to the four walls instead of letting it out in a larger way into Christian television. And you have gotten in touch with the very newspaper that has hated Jim and Tammy the worst, has tried to put PTL under time and time again. You're in an unholy alliance.

"The Word of the Lord [that] is in my mouth is to you, my brother, whom we all love: You're sowing discord, and the Lord says discord will come back to you. Flee, my brother. Repent and ask God to cleanse you.

"You are a good man, and we love you. The Word of the Lord is saying to those people in the headquarters of that denomination where Jim, out of graciousness, turned in his ordination papers because they wanted him to, and you've said, 'No, we're gonna strip him; we're gonna crush him.'

"That's not you. You're better men and women of God than that. Your people across America are grieved. Daily I get calls from ministers in your denomination crying out...that's not the way your movement started. You were a fellowship. You were not an ecclesiastical and [into] legalism, but you gave people freedom. The Word of the Lord is coming from the mouth of...today. If you strip Jim Bakker, you've touched God's anointed, and you've harmed God's Prophet. The Word of the Lord says, 'Touch not mine anointed, and do no harm to my prophets.' A sinking feeling will come upon you, and your countenance will change. You leaders, when you come before your people, there will be something in your face that your people will detect that's not from God. They will turn away from you. I beg you with headquarters of a great denomination, one that we respect and love, desist, move back, and treat Jim Bakker as what he is, an anointed man, a Prophet of God. If you do, the hand of the Lord will not fall upon you, but the Lord will bless you. And the great newspaper, you seem so immune to what our God can do. You've touched God's anointed, and you've tried to harm God's Prophet, Jim Bakker. You've come into an unholy alliance with these others in the name of religion and morality. You've set yourself up to be a standard of morality even though you're not, and you know you're not.

"The Word of the Lord comes unto you from my mouth, and the Lord says He will create great dissension in your ranks. You'll have such dissension that it will spread across the news media of

---

12

America, and you will not know what you're doing. There will be much falling out and falling apart, much anger among yourselves. You will wonder why this happened. Yes, under the First Amendment you have freedom of the press as we have freedom of religion. We respect you; we respect our news media. Of course, we don't like you to take our words out of context and make us suffer. But if we can't bear the persecution, we're not men of God anyway. So we're not running from persecution. We know that God has spoken to us, but we respect your rights in our great pluralistic society...America. Pull away from this unholy alliance.

"The hand of the Lord will fall upon you. You've never known such dissension as that which will come upon you because God said, 'Touch not mine anointed, and do no harm to my prophet.'

"It may appear that men like Oral Roberts, Jim Bakker, and I could call so many others who are just ordinary people because we are just ordinary people. We're just men. We make mistakes. We fall short. We're sorry that we can't be better, but you know the only Man who was ever perfect. They let Him live thirty-three years. They killed Him on a cross. We're not perfect. I've already lived more than twice as long as Christ. Jim Bakker has already lived longer than Jesus, but He was perfect. You want us to be perfect? They would have already killed us. They killed Christ at thirty-three. We are trying to do God's work. We're trying to birth the missionary heart in the Body of Christ.

"We believe that our Jim and Tammy Bakker will be back. We believe it and let's put a wall of protection around Jim and Tammy. Let's reach out in restoration, restoration, restoration."

When the media kept pounding the Bakkers with front page headlines and the Assembly of God headquarters pulled Jim's papers, Oral Roberts made a public apology for this prophecy. Why? Had God made a mistake? Friends, God NEVER makes a mistake! Then why the apology?

Most of us are familiar with the famous Leaning Tower of Pisa in Italy. It leans almost twenty-two feet out of perpendicular. When the architect planned the tower, he designed a 179-foot high structure with only a ten-foot foundation. As a result the tower has leaned for over 800 years. Ingenious schemes have been proposed by various architects to correct the problem. This 14,500-ton tower will fall some day because the foundation lies in soft, watery sub-soil. Those of us without a foundation of balanced Bible teaching will have a leaning "Tower of Pisa" faith. The Word of God is our only authority and assurance not to fall into error.

There are a growing number of people which equate what they say to what God says with the statement, "Thus saith the Lord."

When the infallibility of the Bible is denied, every Bible doctrine is in danger of being destroyed.

The written Word of God is conclusive.

If someone says, "I have a new revelation from God," do not believe him. The Bible has NO new chapters. In II Peter 1:20, 21 we read: "For no prophecy recorded in Scripture was ever thought up by the prophet himself. It was the Holy Spirit within these godly men who gave them true messages from God." (LB)

The Bible was written by forty different authors in a span of about 1,500 years. Many of these authors wrote in several languages about hundreds of topics. They were not even acquainted.

The inerrant inspired Bible we cherish is

1. The Imparted Word
2. The Revealed Word
3. The Preserved Word
4. The United Word
5. The Conclusive Word
6. The Transforming Word

The written Word of God is without error. It is true, the

Bible records errors or false statements said by others. One such statement is the serpent's lying to Eve, and she believed the lie that God would not punish her for disobedience. (Gen. 3:4)

"God, Himself, is free from error; this is the clear testimony of the Scriptures. It is wholly consistent to believe that the Scriptures are provided to help us avoid error. And we are wholly inconsistent with God if we vary from the written Word of God in the revelation of the truths of God conveyed by inspiration through His servants to us as such; it is the infallible Word of God." (Author Unknown)

The Bible claims for Itself, Verbal Inspiration. Some people would tell us "the thoughts are inspired, but not the words." This could not be true, for a thought is a group of spoken words.

Jesus referred to Verbal Inspiration in Matthew 5:18: "For verily I say unto you, till heaven and earth pass, one jot or one tittle shall in no wise pass from the law, till all be fulfilled."

Verse 17 makes it clear that the law refers to the entire Scripture. Why is the written Word of God, our Bible, so dependable? Why does this book qualify for our final authority? In Luke 24:27 we read: "And beginning at Moses and all the prophets, he expounded unto them in all the scriptures the things concerning himself."

Jesus either cites or refers to the Old Testament more than 400 times and this He did without any question or hesitation. He stamped the canon of the Old Testament with His imprimatur, in His conversation with the two disciples in Luke 24.

In the Bible we are given twelve titles for the Word. They are:

1. *The Word of God*, for all the authority of the God of the Word is behind it (Matt. 4:4).
2. *The Word of the Lord*, for the Lord of the Word is its Author and Owner (Acts 8:25).
3. *The Word of this Salvation*, for the salvation is proclaimed in it (Acts 13:26).

4. *The Word of the Gospel*, for resurrection and power are heralded by it (Acts 15:7).

5. *The Word of His Grace*, for his grace like a river flows through it (Acts 20:32).

6. *The Word of Faith*, for faith is created by means of it (Romans 10:8).

7. *The Word of Reconciliation*, for reconciliation to God is its message (II Cor. 5:19).

8. *The Word of Truth*, for truth is revealed by it (II Cor. 6:7).

9. *The Word of Life*, for life come through it (Philippians 2:16).

10. *The Word of Righteousness*, for it is a rule by which we square the life (Heb. 5:13).

11. *The Good Word of God*, for God's goodness is promised in it (Heb. 6:5).

12. *The Sure Word of Prophecy*, for the Holy Spirit assures by it (II Peter 1:19) and many more.

The entire seventeenth chapter of John is the longest recorded prayer in all of the Bible. It was Christ's prayer. I quote verses 14-17: "I have given them thy word; and the world hath hated them, because they are not of the world, even as I am not of the world. I pray not that thou shouldest take them out of the world, but that thou shouldest keep them from the evil. They are not of the world, even as I am not of the world. Sanctify them through thy truth: thy word is truth."

The last four words of this text are the basis of our belief in the reliability of the Scripture. The Scripture is not human counsel; it is the truth of Divine counsel. It is as absolute as it is timeless. "FOR EVER, O LORD, THY WORD IS SETTLED IN HEAVEN." (Psalm 119:89)

When Paul stood to speak, he would unroll the scrolls and point out the truth. He preached what Moses had written as well as Jeremiah and Amos. Paul, in I Thessalonians 2:13, says: "And for this reason we also constantly thank God that when you received from us the word of God's message, you accepted it not as the word of men, but for what it really is, the word of God, which also performs its work in you who believe.'' (NAS)

If Jesus came back to speak to our world today, His words would agree and be harmonious with the Scripture. His opinion, counsel, commands, desires, warnings, and His very mind is the WRITTEN WORD OF GOD. I Peter 1:25 says: "But the word of the Lord abides forever. And this is the word which was preached to you.'' (NAS)

In II Peter 1:21 we read: "For the prophecy came not in old time by the will of man: but holy men of God spake as they were moved by the Holy Ghost.''

The English word "moved" is translated from an ancient Greek nautical term. It describes a ship at sea. When a ship loses its power to move, it is at the mercy of the sea. It remains a ship, but it was without its own power or energy.

This word "moved" referred not to ships at sea, but men who wrote (in their own style). They did not write out of their own intellect, power, and will, but by the Holy Spirit.

Old Testament Scripture is all true! Every word, every thought, and every grammatical phrasing is involved in inspiration.

The inspiration of the Bible is complete. There is not any part of the Scripture that is without full doctrinal authority. Luke 16:17 says, "And it is easier for heaven and earth to pass, than one tittle of the law to fail.''

The written Word of God is "more" than "Ink On Paper.'' The neo-orthodox view says, "God's Written Word is petrified in a dead record until you and I encounter It, and It becomes alive.'' They say, "God never did really speak propositionally in the WORD; God speaks personally in private revelation when we encounter Him.'' To say that God speaks to us in private revelation is true. But the statement is inconclusive, for when God speaks to us in private, He speaks to our heart, out of His written Word. For the neo-orthodox to state that God never did speak out of His written Word is HERESY. The written Word of God becomes "knowledge" only when the Holy Spirit applies that "Word" to our hearts (Rhema). The Holy Spirit will apply only the written Word of God - and nothing more.

The Holy Spirit transforms our lives today through His Word, the Bible. A former surgeon-general of Portugal was out walking one rainy day. When he returned to his home, he found a piece of paper sticking to his shoe. When he pulled it off, he discovered it to be a tract that presented the Gospel by using Scripture. On reading it, he was soundly converted because the written Word of God became knowledge to him.

To assume extra-biblical revelation is "error!" God's revelations are not private in the sense that what He reveals will be "new" truth. God's revelation will not be strange or contrary to His written Word. A revelation can be "new" to us as individuals in the sense that the truth has been revealed to us personally for the first time.

The Bible is the only literature I read, THAT READS ME. I have read John Bunyan's Pilgrim's Progress, hymns, poetry, sermons, and many songs; however, no literature TRANSFORMS, except THE WORD OF GOD applied, by the Holy Spirit, to the heart of man.

It is sacrilegious to compare cheap, flaunty words of men to THE WRITTEN WORD OF GOD. R.G. Lee said, "Since the Bible is revelation of the all wise and unchanging God, it appears audacious to attempt to improve it. God's Word is not a nose of wax to be shaped by the fingers of fashion."

Jeremiah 23:16-18 and 21-22 gives us a warning: "...Don't listen to these false prophets when they prophesy to you, filling you with futile hopes. They are making up everything they say. They do not speak for me! They keep saying to these rebels who despise me, 'Don't worry! All is Well'; and those who live the way they want to, 'The Lord has said you shall have peace!' But can you name even one of these prophets who lives close enough to God to hear what He is saying? Has even one of them cared enough to listen? I have not sent these prophets, yet they claim to speak for me; I gave them no message, yet they say their words are mine. If they were mine, they would try to turn my people from their evil ways." (LB)

The "God told me to tell you" syndrome did not spring up in just the past few years. Hundreds of sects and cults are based on a portion of the Bible. The scheme of Satan has always been to question, add to, or to dilute, the written Word of God.

If you say, "God told me to tell you" you had better be telling the truth and nothing but the truth, so help you God! And that "Truth" must be the WRITTEN WORD OF GOD!

The Word of God has not changed since it was written. Author Loyd C. Douglas used to tell how he loved to visit an old man who gave violin lessons. The old man had a kind of homely wisdom that refreshed him. One morning Douglas walked in and said, "Well, what's the good news today?"

The old man put down his violin and stepped over to a tuning fork suspended from a cord. He struck it a smart blow and said, "There's the good news for today; that, my friend, is the musical note 'A.' It was 'A' all day yesterday, and it will be 'A' next week and for a thousand years."

Praise God we can proclaim, "For ever, O Lord, thy word is settled in heaven." (Psalm 119:89)

Paul constantly avoided proclaiming the Word of God like the wandering apostles of that day. They were presenting their own spiritual power by drawing impressive words and preaching with mixed motives modifying and falsifying God's word. Paul says in II Corinthians 2:17, "For we are not as many, which corrupt the word of God: but as of sincerity, but as of God, in the sight of God speak we in Christ."

The story is told of a man selling apple butter and clabber milk. He was working out of two crock pots, one on each side. He was using the same ladle to dip into both pots. Business was good, and he had dipped into them many times during the day. Before the day was over, his customers could not tell if they were buying apple butter or clabber milk. They were getting the strange mixture of the two.

The strange concoction being propagated today is man's own self-serving ideas. Special revelations and half-truths and murky renderings of the Scripture emerging as a special revelation from God is dangerous.

Error ranges from the Jim Jones style of fraud to those who move in and out of prayer groups, to big time exploiting on television. Even church denominations are questioning the infallibility of the written Word of God. Someone has said,

"Old Error In New Dress, is Ever Error None The Less."

Any attempt to add to what God has said, whether utterance, vision, dream, or prophecy will potentially result in cults, heresy, and the weakening of the body of Christ. The fraud that is being propagated in these last days is appalling.

The Reformers guarded Christianity from extra-biblical errors, with the cry..."SOLA SCRIPTURA" (Scripture only). In this day when many are suggesting "SCRIPTURE PLUS..." or "I have a special word of knowledge for you," let's insist "Sola Scriptura." If we do not insist on God's Written Word only, we will continue to see theological chaos and spiritual disaster.

To verbally forge God's name to our religious babbling is what the prophet spoke of in Ezekiel 13:3, 8: "Thus saith the Lord God; Woe unto the foolish prophets, that follow their own spirit, and have seen nothing! Because you have spoken vanity, and seen lies, therefore, behold, I am against you, saith the Lord God."

Peter warns that false prophets will "exploit" with stories they have made up. The Greek word "emporos" is translated "exploit" which is a commercial connotation. Peter seems to have in mind those who prophesy lies to reap financial gain. Anyone who declares "THUS SAITH THE LORD" is a false prophet, if God did not say it first. (II Peter 2:1-3)

You cannot gild gold, paint rubies, and brighten diamonds. No artist can add any finished touch to the Written Word of God. It stands as the sun in the sky. Any addition that man may attempt to make will be only a patch and a disappointment.

II Peter 1:20 says, "...no prophecy of the Scripture is of any private interpretation," or "springs out of any prophet's devising or unfolding. It is not a mere human prognostication." (My version)

The Bible is a revelation from the Holy Spirit.

Jeremiah's words are a straight-to-the-point accusation against self-appointed prophets. " 'Yes,' declares the Lord, 'I am against the prophets who wag their own tongues and yet declare, 'The Lord declares.' Indeed, I am against those who prophesy false dreams,' declares the Lord. 'They tell them and lead my people astray with their reckless lies, yet I did not send or appoint them. They do not benefit these people in the least,' declares the Lord.'' (Jeremiah 23:31, 32) (NIV) SOLA SCRIPTURA!

2

SMORGASBORD'S "GOD TOLD ME-"

People all over the country are running around using "God told me" to get their own way or wield power. The following article is a classic example.

"DEAR ANN LANDERS: I am married to a minister in North Carolina. Please do not print the name of the city. He would kill me.

"The problem is my husband. Whenever I ask him to do something that he doesn't want to do, he says, "I spoke to God, and He said I shouldn't do it." I wish the man would have the decency to say straight out that he doesn't want to do something instead of laying it on the back of the Lord.

"I haven't seen my mother in three years. I told my husband last week that I wanted to go visit her. Well, he prayed over it and God told him this wasn't the right time. It WAS the right time, however, for him to treat fifteen friends to lunch in a nice restaurant while I stayed home and cooked for twenty-two Girl Scouts.

"God tells my husband when to play golf and when to go fishing. He has also instructed him to go to some beautiful vacation spots (alone) so he can meditate and pray.

"I know I need counseling, but a minister's wife isn't supposed to have any problems, and I am afraid that it might reflect poorly on my husband if I went for help. In this town everybody knows everybody else's business.

"Just writing this letter has made me feel better. Thanks for being there. And, please tell me what to do, Ann." Stymied and Stuck in a No-Name Place

"Dear S & S: Get some counseling, woman! Ministers' wives need it just as much (if not more) than other wives.

"Make plans at once to visit your mother. Tell your husband you wrote to me, and I consulted with the Lord. He quoted the commandment that says, "Honor thy father and thy mother," and I decided you should honor your mother with a visit right away."

This sort of "God Told Me To Tell You" is the standard evasion. Assortment is the fashion in Religion today. You can select anything you want. Whatever suits your taste, Satan makes available. There are the Moonies, Jim Jones, and the wheelers and dealers. They deal in sawdust, oil, jars of honey, and gimmick letters. These are the get-rich-quick positive thinkers, screaming showmen with healing lines who offer a built-in guarantee.

The same gullible people who would not fall for someone's saying, "I am God" take the bait of Satan's most dangerous fraud, "GOD TOLD ME TO TELL YOU."

To illustrate: few people in America would be fooled by Guru Maharai Ji who claims to be a true avatar, a living incantation of God.

There are good things in this god's life. The $100,000 townhouse in London, the private jets, yachts, and airline stewardess - to mention a few.

The highest of this incarnation came at the Houston Astrodome in the fall of 1973, when Maharai Ji kicked off the millennium, billed as the most holy and significant event in human history.

Abbie Hoffman is not so fond of the Guru as his fellow Chicago Seven defendant. "If the Guru Maharai Ji is God," he groused, "He's the kind of god America deserves."

It is often true in religion, that the "Talk" is greater than the "Walk." Several years ago a carload of us preachers, coming from a meeting stopped in front of a religious headquarters named "The Voice of Healing." One of the preachers remarked, "More voice than healing."

The big talks and boasting we see in some ranks in religion is like the worst Horatio Alger story. Alger told this himself. He made a fortune writing one hundred nineteen books on rags to riches. He was a notorious spendthrift and died totally destitute. So it often is in religion. We end up in spiritual rags after having talked "big" results!

When a person says to you, "God told me to tell you," what is the appropriate response? What protection does one have against the self serving prophet with an exploiting spirit? The only safeguard to protect the innocent from a self-styled prophet on a "mind trip" is the approved balanced knowledge of God's Word. Only then can we stand before God unashamed.

The reason for discretion about personal prophecies is that young, wobbly Christians are damaged by the Charismatic Fortune-Tellers armed with the spirit of "snooping" and suspicion.

THE DILEMMA OF THE 'GOD TOLD ME TO TELL YOU' SYNDROME!

The "con" is possible because the prophet says he receives this "Word of Knowledge" direct from God, and in many cases it cannot be proved or disproved. Such was the occasion when a well known TV preacher said, "There is a woman in Kansas City who has sinus. The Lord is drying that up right now. Thank you, Jesus. There is a woman in Cincinnati with cancer of the lymph nodes..."

Who can prove or disprove this prophecy that many receive as a Word direct from God?

In 1986, soon after the full importance of the Aids epidemic began to become evident, the same evangelist was attempting to cure it. He invoked God's power: "We rebuke this virus and we command your immune system to work in the name of Jesus."

In over thirty-four years of pastoring, I have observed many instances of this type of prophecy. Both laity and leadership of varied religions are mixed up in this handicap.

EXAMPLES OF THE "GOD TOLD ME...," SYNDROME

According to Pat Robertson, God told him to stay out of politics. In his 1972 autobiography, *Shout It From The Housetops*, the Republican Presidential hopeful wrote that in 1966 he did not campaign for his father, a U.S. Senator from Virginia, because God told him not to. A passage on page 195 of the 1972 paperback edition reads, " 'I have called you to My ministry,' He spoke to my heart. 'You cannot tie My eternal purposes to the success of any political candidate...not even your father.' "

However, the "God-told-me-to-stay-out-of-politics passage" was cut from a glossy, hardback of the book issued last October, 1987 to commemorate the 25th Anniversary of Robertson's Christian Broadcasting Network.

*   *   *   *   *

One well-known pastor scatters through his sermon the statement that the "Lord is speaking to me concerning etc." He says, "There is someone here with a crick in his neck."

This type of revelation is common. During the time this "prophet" was exercising his "Word of knowledge," he was exposed as an active homosexual.

Larry Lea, a pastor of a large charismatic church in Rockwell, Texas is reported to state to his congregation that, "The Lord shows me, etc." He is speaking to the twenty-five families that morning who were joining his church. The church has a weekly attendance of over five thousand.

To increase the membership of the church certainly is not wrong, but to say the Lord was telling the pastor that twenty-five people were to join the church is secular. Church-joining is entirely man's idea. It is nice and needful as many things we do. However, why would we need a special revelation from the Lord through a preacher to tell us "This is the day to join a church"?

Just another gimmick propped up with a "God told me to tell you."

* * * * *

A married man, in a church, confessed to an adulterous affair he was having with a married woman in the same congregation. They said that God had sanctioned their sin. This, like most "God told me revelations" is self- serving.

* * * * *

In the church nursery, a mother rocked her baby as she spoke of her divorce. She admitted with a smile and a shrug, "We knew we were doing wrong having affairs, but we knew God would forgive us."

To be victims of divorce is one thing, but to walk into adultery with the excuse that "God understands" is unsound. Using God's grace to serve "self," assured that God will forgive, is presumptuous to say the least.

* * * * *

"Convicted police killer Thomas Andy Barefoot was executed October 30, 1984. The former roughneck from Iberia, LA was pronounced dead at 12:24 a.m. Texas Governor Mark White refused to grant him a 30-day reprieve. Barefoot

repeatedly said God would intervene and spare his life."
(News, Huntsville, TX)

This impression he received and verbalized was nothing more than a "wish" and one can sympathize. Probably, Barefoot did believe that God would spring him. His "special revelation" and intense desire to live is the substance of many "God told me to tell you" statements.

* * * * *

A wife, who was beaten often by her husband said, "Pastor, why does this happen to me? I have tried so hard, but I take it from him." Her husband had beat her severely, at times when he was intoxicated. She said, "I thought he was trying to kill me." Her explanation was, "God told me to take the abuse and because of my submission he would eventually come to God."

Poor old God getting the blame again. God must not be blamed for wife-beating. A battered wife's excusing her weakness by saying, "God told me to take it" is nothing more than a cop-out to not stand against wrong. Not one of the twelve to fifteen million women abused each year has God's stamp of approval.

* * * * *

Christians are not the only people who blame God. Tiny Tim the long-haired, high-voiced entertainer said, "God told me I wasn't like anybody else. The Spirit of the Lord touched me, telling me to sing in a high voice. I felt I had something and wasn't like anybody else."

* * * * *

Many of the things blamed on God are ridiculous, yet humorous. A pastor friend related the following to me: "A lady said God told her to drop their car insurance. Her husband, an insurance agent, was also urged to trust the Lord for insurance coverage. In time, a rock hit their windshield. The damage caused a bad crack about the size of a baseball. She would not be denied and began to believe for restoration of the windshield. Eventually she admitted the break had not completely disappeared. However, through their prayers and faith she claimed the smashed area had reduced down to about the size of a pea. When and if God chooses to restore a windshield or anything else, He will, according to His track record, complete the project.

The following is a classic example of Charismatic Fortune- Telling. (Transcribed from a television program in October, 1985)

> An evangelist, speaking to a young man taken from the audience, says: "I hear you saying, 'Lord I want to worship You,' I hear you saying 'Father, not my will, Thine be done'...in fact...have you???...have you been praying about moving?..somewhere...orrr...ah...ah...it's almost like saying 'Lord if you want me to go to Tim Buck Two...if that's where You lead, I'm ready to go.' "

> At this point the young man breaks into heavy crying. The evangelist continues: "Brother, God has heard your prayer, and the Lord said you're gonna be led by His Spirit. God said He's gonna anoint your hands. God said He's gonna lay them on the sick, and they're gonna be made whole. God said He's gonna anoint your lips to speak with the power of the Holy Spirit...I want to say something about...Keith?"

> The young man becomes extremely emotional again, hands sticking straight into the air, and says: "That's my name; that's my name!" (End of television segment)

The appropriate statement for this type of operation is "fakery."

* * * * *

A prominent lawyer in our city received an evangelist's promotional material. The instructions were, "Go into your bathroom, take this string, and form a circle on the floor. Get inside the circle. Then take the anointing oil, anoint your billfold, then anoint your largest bill, and send it to me."

The letter from the TV Evangelist closes with, "Now I have obeyed God."

This bizarre type of gimmick is presented as a special word from God. It is a small percent of the suggestible people who fall for that flimsy trick. Some apparently do not know the difference between the "real" and the "counterfeit," or religious crooks could not continue to operate.

*　*　*　*　*

An itinerate preacher holds services in the banquet room of a local motel. The following is recorded from one of his services. The preacher kept proclaiming that "The light keeps coming out of my mouth."

He is speaking the Word of God; he says, "The light is shooting out from behind me." He states, "I am going invisible right before their eyes."

It is reported that some people see this light, and some do not. The evangelist states, "Those that cannot see the light are not ready to go in the rapture."

On one occasion, "Jesus came and sat in a chair. He sat there in the flesh for ten or fifteen minutes, I believe. See my eyes light up," He says. "You cannot get the Holy Ghost on video, but you can record it and it can be seen only by the spiritual. When the video is played back, it doesn't show the phenomenon of light," He explained. "You can't trap the Holy Ghost on film," but you can record a flimflam preacher on a cassette.

*　*　*　*　*

In Kentucky some people founded a unique nudist church and campground. One of their group had a vision. He heard the Holy Spirit say, "Go home and take off your

---

30

clothes, and tell the family to do the same thing."

The brother, Bennie, came from Texas to "See the glories of God revealed. I have preached all over Florida and saw people healed when they disrobed and prayed." (Deceitful workers) (II Cor. 11:13-15)

* * * * *

A friend of a family in our church fell under the influence of some self appointed "prophets" in our city. One of the mini-prophets in this charismatic prayer group gave a personal prophecy over this lady. He announced that she was pregnant, and the date of birth was prophesied to be nine months from the time of the prophecy. The baby was due in the spring. There was no reason to believe the lady was pregnant, except for the testimony of those who believed the prophecy. At the end of the nine months, they met with the woman. They heated water, preparing for a mid-wife type delivery. After a "no show" one of them said, "Oh shucks if she is not going to have a baby, let's use that water for instant coffee." She didn't; they did.

* * * * *

A computer letter from TV evangelist W.V. Grant, Jr. reads as follows:

"Dear Joe Bryant,

"I called your name in prayer at Jesus' tomb, in the upper room, and a third time in the Garden of Gethsemane. I had a dream about you Tuesday night, while in Jerusalem. You were in (computer placed the name of town). In this dream, I never saw your face...just your beautiful glowing hand and name, "Brother Joe Bryant." Mark 11:24 was written across your chest. Your shirt was red and white." (Then the appeal for money follows.)

II Corinthians 11:20 reads, "In fact, you even put up with anyone who enslaves you or exploits you or takes advantage of you or pushes himself forward or slaps you in the face." (NIV)

31

The reason for including all of these off-beat incidents is to point out that they are all un-scriptural. Though many erie incidents have no scriptural foundation, many of God's people insist on falling for the "God told me to tell you" suggestions. It is heart-rendering to see peoples mouths wide open like little birds swallowing anything that is fed to them, even poison.

*   *   *   *   *

About mid-point of a Gospel-singing performance, one of our guest singers gave out a supposed word of knowledge. A young couple in the congregation were all eyes and ears, taking in everything. The lady, pointing to the couple, said something to this effect: "I see travel... suitcases... err... ah... I'm not for sure... the Lord has great things in store for you, etc...."

The essence of her words was that God was calling this couple into the ministry. After the service they asked me what they should do. I advised them to go and work for the Lord in their own church. And I reminded them that God very seldom ordains people into the ministry one day and expects them to be full-time ministers the next day.

Some may ask, "Was the lady's prophecy the word of knowledge?" No, for this was a reading about a personality, not "a Word (Logos) of knowledge" (God's word made real). "Was it an occult experience?" No, it was a mind trip. The person was a deceived super-spiritual, making an off-the cuff prophecy. However, the effect of this fortune-telling could have resulted in the couple's entering the ministry not approved or called of God.

The Word of God warns us in I John 4:1, "Dearly loved friends, don't always believe everything you hear just because someone says it is a message from God: test it first to see if it really is. For there are many false teachers around." (LB)

Are these "God told me to tell you" people expert con artists or honest deceived leaders of God? The crowd consists of both but, whatever the case, it is "error."

Some TV evangelists will set you straight on political

issues and medical problems. Another preacher says, "Send money and you will have health, prosperity, a better job, expensive cars, and etc."

God is presented as a cosmic bellhop, summoned by a buzzer of prayer.

America apparently has not seen her fill of rip-offs and hucksters. Shysters abound for there is always someone to keep them in business. The percentage of Americans that fall for T.V. and Tent-type Preachers is the minority. However, the number of gullible people is multitudinous.

*   *   *   *   *

Paul tells us that discernment is one characteristic that accompanies genuine spirituality. (I Cor. 2:14-16)

Hebrews 5:14 calls it a mark of maturity. The Greek word here is "diakrisis" (clear discrimination), the phrase consisting of pros with this noun; lit, "towards a discerning," is translated "To discern," said of those who are capable of discriminating between good and evil. The discriminating between "good" and "evil" is not an imitation reading of a personality as that of a palm reader or any type of prognosticator. It is the Christian telling the difference between "good" and "evil."

In I Corinthians 12:10 we read, "...to another discerning of spirits..." (diakrisis, distinguishing a clear discrimination, discerning, judging of spirits by evidence whether they are evil or of God.)

The person with a balanced knowledge of the written Word of God, led by the Holy Spirit, will discern whether the "spirit" emitting from a person is from God or Satan.

This maturity and spirituality comes from the knowledge we receive from God's written Word applied by the Holy Spirit. One grounded in the Word of God, a life style bathed in prayer and led by the Holy Spirit will discern between "good" and "evil." This "discernment" is not a "super spiritual" status that permits a few to read things in other people's life or mind.

Discernment picks and chooses with care. Every believer

discerns. Look at John's counsel: "Beloved, do not put faith in every spirit, but prove (test) the spirits to discover whether they proceed from God..." (I John 4:1) (Amplified Bible)

In today's language John is saying, "discern, stop believing everything you hear."

John's admonition is for each of us to "discern" not to turn psychic.

A dangerous comment about some spiritual leaders is "I did what he said...for God speaks to him directly. He saw a vision about me..." or "He had a word of knowledge, and it was for me." This is error. Your word must come from God!

All "deceitful workers" are not on street corners selling little magazines. Many are supported by the credentials of intelligence. They are popular, impressive in appearance, yet charlatans, religious fakes, and masters of deceit. The media serves them under your nose. Their beautiful attractive books, luxurious headquarters, nationwide TV shows, and success stories add credence to their "message."

The following is an account from the book *Power Evangelism* by John Wimber with Kevin Springer, Harper & Row.

> Written across his face in very clear and distinct letters I thought I saw the word 'adultery.' I blinked, rubbed my eyes, and looked again. It was still there. 'Adultery.' I was seeing it not with my eyes, but my minds eyes. No one else was on the plane. I am sure I saw it. It was the Spirit of God communicating to me. The fact that it was a spiritual phenomenon made it no less real.
>
> Somewhat nervously, I leaned across the aisle and asked, "Does the name Jane (not her real name) mean anything to you?"
>
> He looked at me suspiciously for a moment, then asked, "Who told you that name?"
>
> "God told me," I blurted out. I was too rattled to think of a way to ease into the topic more gracefully.
>
> "God told you?" He almost shouted the question, he was so shocked by what I had said.

"Yes," I answered, taking a deep breath. "He also told me to tell you...that unless you turn from this adulterous relationship, He is going to take your life."

(A video was also produced to promote this book.)

There are approximately twenty people on stage waiting for prayer as Wimber says, "When we turn to look at a group of people like this, we are looking for indications of the Father's working on the individual. And when we see, either distinguishing of spirits or through natural means, the Spirit of God already moving on somebody, that's the first person we would go and minister to.

"We do that because of the basic assumption that we should do what the Father is doing." (Wimber points to a person being prayed for by one of the team)..."can you see the energy on his body?" (The man is shaking.) "You see that spasming that's going on is involuntary. It's just power. Remember the eyes are the windows of the soul, and sometimes when we are moving in the Spirit of God will contract and contact someone else. Can you see that happening here?" (pointing to the man with spasms). "Now look at the lady. The same thing's happening to her. And all it is, operationally: they are yielding to something that they feel happening in them." (end of video)

These comments are alarming. Wimber says he is "looking for indications of the Father working on an individual...through distinguishing of the spirits or through natural means, that's the person we go to... You can see the energy on his body... You see that spasm going on involuntarily?...They are yielding to something they feel happening to them."

Wimber's evaluation of these physical reactions are more

mystic in nature rather than Godly worship. What he here describes can be seen at any rock concert or by observing Shamen in their frenzy worship to Satan. A word of knowledge or discernment is very unlikely. What happened to his subjects does not describe a spiritual faith experience. The un-yielding and scriptural fact is that Wimber did not speak a "Word of Knowledge" (I Cor. 12:8). Only the Holy Spirit speaks Rhema.

On one occasion God gave Pat the "word" that He had just healed a woman's broken ankle. It was later discovered that the video healing was performed three weeks before the woman's ankle was broken. The video was delayed three weeks before airing on the stations across America. Such discrepancies mean nothing to the people who do not follow closely the Word. They are accustomed to this type of logic.

All of these bizarre happenings: stripping off clothes, battering wives, a red string for healing, and calling someone's sins and names are ploys that work only on misguided individuals. This is how fortune-tellers, pseudo seers, mediums, and so-called divine healers mulct (milk) the millions. Hard-earned dollars are raked from the gullible every year, by deceitful workers.

This chapter could not be ended with more appropriate words than those from Isaiah 30:10 where the prophet reveals the attitude of the spiritually naive: "Give us no more vision of what is right. Tell us pleasant things, prophesy illusions."

People not properly rooted in the Truth will always be around, for there are so *few students of the Word*. Collossians 2:18, 19 hits the target about Charismatic Fortune-Telling: "...Such a person goes into great detail about what he has seen, and his unspiritual mind puffs him up with idle notions. He has lost connection with the Head..." (NIV)

The answer that God has for those who ask, "What is the Lord's answer or What has He spoken?" is Jeremiah 23:36, "But you must not mention the 'oracle of the Lord' again, because every man's own word becomes his oracle and so you distort the words of the Living God, the Lord Almighty, our God." (NIV)

3

THE SPIRIT OF ERROR

Teaching an error would not be so dangerous, if it was not mixed with truth. Error is truth out of balance!

Jesus said, "Ye do err, not knowing the scriptures..." (Matthew 22:29) (KJV)

"Error is so nearly alloyed to truth, that it blends with it as imperceptibly as the colors of the rainbow fade into each other." - W.B. Clulow

"In every religious error which has gained a footing in the world there is some mixture of truth. Absolute error, falsehood with no mixture of truth, would contradict man's sense of what is just and right too violently, it would not be sufficiently plausible, its leaden weight of absurdity would sink it. There must be some fragment of truth attached in order to make it float and in nothing has the craft of Satan and of his agents been more conspicuous than in the sagacity with which they mix a maximum of falsehood with a minimum of truth." - L.H. Wiseman.

From 1982-1987 religious T.V. shows have increased forty- eight percent. This is according to the National Religious Broadcasters' Organization in Morrison Town, N.J. If you watch two hours of electronic church a day, you'll be asked for more than $135,000 in a year. Some of the money goes for good deeds, limousines, mansions for ministers. Some has even been used to pay hush money and to hire prostitutes.

Many have been told by the "modern day prophets," "You are being healed" or "blessed" in some unusual way. Yet these prayers or statements were not answered as the evangelists prophesied. What is being promised is not true. All do not get new jobs; kids do not always come home; and separated couples do not always reunite, for God still gives man his free will. These promises are projected in a positive manner: "If you have the faith, then you can order exactly what you desire." It is the old Chevrolet or Cadillac faith philosophy.

The impression is created that, "If you really believe, the cancer cells will change. If you do not have the faith, you die!" This is an injustice to all those dying people who have been told "You are healed," by a lying preacher. Ezekiel 13:6, 9 states, "They have spoken falsehood and divined a lie; they say, 'Says the Lord,' when the Lord has not sent them, and yet they expect him to fulfill their word...My hand will be against the prophets who see delusive visions and who give lying divinations; they shall not be in the council of my people, nor be enrolled in the register of the house of Israel, nor shall they enter the land of Israel; and you shall know that I am the Lord God." (RSV)

Transcribed from a successful television program were the words of Robert Tilton:

> "One of the ways that God speaks to me is through dreams. Every now and then, I will have a vision, a slight vision, but it talks about this in the book of Acts that in the last days, God is going to pour out His spirit upon all flesh, and sons and daughters will prophesy, old men will have dreams, and young men will have visions...I have dreams from time to time, and several years ago I had a

dream and in that dream I saw a multitude of people in front of me but yet they were in front of me one at a time. And I heard the Lord. He was about maybe thirty feet behind me and like He was up in the air. I don't know if He was tall or what, but I know He was about sixty feet behind me. And this is the way it happened. And I looked to these people, and they are hurting. I have never seen so many problems, sicknesses, diseases, and fear. The power of darkness just had them bound. And I heard the voice of the Lord speak to me, and He said these words: 'Many of my ministers pray for my people, but I want you to pray the prayer of AGREEMENT . . .!'

"Oh!...there's a presence of the Lord right now, see, I can help you and I'm bold and I know, I know, I know that what, I know, and I know that I can help you --- if you will only listen to this program, and I mean really listen.

"I can help you today because I am sent by God, by the Spirit of God to you. Those of you who has some kind of problems, God has anointed me to help people break the mountain of problems down --- to pull them down. I know that I know what I know! And I know according to Isaiah [must have been a reference to Isaiah 49:1]. 'Listen, O isles, unto me; and hearken, ye people, from far; The Lord hath called me from the womb; from the bowels of my mother hath he made mention of my name.'

"If you will listen to me, I can help you...I know how to release the abundant supply of God into your life. I know how; it is not hype. I'm talking about what I have found in God's Word that will produce results in your life . . .''

(The evangelist begins to prophesy over television with his head bowed and his eyes squeezed closed. He carries on with the following "typical" charismatic fortune-telling.)

"John, or whatever his name, Bill, does not know what to do. You have just got through talking about that. You don't know what God's will is for you. If you've got this desire in you, you know, there is a stirring, (there's someone right there) you've got a stirring in your being, God has something coming for you'll...YOU NEED TO SEND FOR IT TODAY, A 1,000 dollars, you need to send for whatever it is. If this is you, you need to release your faith today for $1,000. 'You say how do you know I'm supposed to?'

"I know this: The Bible says, 'Believe His prophets and so shall ye prosper.' I know this: that God has already spoken to you, the figure. Even if He hadn't, if you will act on the anointed Word, you will partake of it and GOD WILL HAVE TO MOVE IN YOUR LIFE, A BOLDNESS COMES, AND KEEPS THE ENEMY FROM STEALING YOUR SEED BECAUSE YOU GET INTO EXPECTANCY."

(The evangelist again begins to pray:)

"Somebody's mountain is going to be removed today. God gave me faith for ears the other days, just dropped into my head like backs, quickly lay your hands on the T.V. screen, come on lay your hand on the screen.

"We are going off the air, those of you that was just ministered to, you need to offer a thanksgiving offering, SOMEONE GAVE $500 THE OTHER DAY. YOU NEED TO GIVE $1,000 TODAY BECAUSE YOU DIDN'T DO WHAT GOD TOLD YOU TO DO THE FIRST TIME. There it is again. God told you a different figure, and you haven't done it. You need to do...it's better to obey God than to obey man.

"Now I'm going to prophesy over these requests and release the miracle power of God into your life. Father, right now I decree miracles in the name of Jesus." (End of prophecy)

Jeremiah, plain-spoken, denounces the above man-energized, self-serving prophecy. Lamentations 2:14 and 3:37, 38 states, "The visions of your prophets were false and worthless; they did not expose your sin to ward off your captivity. The oracles they gave you were false and misleading...Who can speak and have it happen if the Lord has not decreed it? Is it not from the mouth of the Most High that both calamities and good things come?" (NIV)

A Christian, balanced in the Word of God, led by the Spirit will discern that these kinds of prophesies are from the "spirit of error".

The preacher looks good, sounds spiritual and has a multi- million dollar program. You get the feeling this one may be legitimate - until he begins his, "God told me to tell you."

Apparently the primary purpose of the evangelist's prophecy was raising money. His prayers and commands for miracles are nothing but absolute demands of God to send money to him. Many will not fall for the pitch; however, thousands do send checks, cash, diamonds, etc. Air time alone costs the electronic church millions. Thus, the need for much emotion and promotion. Most people who support T.V. ministries are not involved in a local church. They seek the services of the church for weddings, baby dedications, funerals, etc..., yet the thousands who give to these tele-evangelists could help more people and save more souls if they would give that money to their local Gospel-preaching church. Titus 1:11 states, "They must be silenced, because they are ruining whole households by teaching things they ought not to teach - and that for the sake of dishonest gain." (NIV)

Even if the money the masses send is not used for financial gain or illegal purposes, it would be better spent through the local church where one can see where the money is going. The Bible teaches us to "bring the tithe," not to send it. God's basic plan is the local church!

I Timothy 6:3-5 proclaims, "If anyone teaches false doctrines and does not agree...to godly teaching...who have been robbed of the truth and who think that godliness is a means to financial gain.'' (NIV)

When we see and hear operations, like the T.V. program just described, we are reminded that error is never so dangerous as when it is mixed with truth.

"Error is of a spreading nature; it is compared to leaven, because it sours, (Matt. 16:11), and gangrene, because it spreads, (II Tim. 2:17). One error seldom goes alone. Error spreads from one person to another; it is like the plague, which infects all round about. Satan by infecting one person with error, infects more.'' - WATSON

Pure error is likely to be rejected but error mixed with truth makes use of truth as a pioneer. Error gets introduction where otherwise it would have none. Poison is never so dangerous than when it is mixed with delicious food. Men twist the Scripture, and that opens the door to error.

In one simple statement, error is that which is not totally sanctioned by the Written Word of God.

Most Christians reject the idea that knocking on wood guarantees good luck and refuse the idea that a Quija board can spell out one's future.

It is confounding that these same people will fall for the gimmicks of the "Charismatic Fortune-Teller!"

We accept the laying on of hands for healing, communion, and water baptism because they are scriptural.

Oral and Richard Roberts recently dipped water out of their man-made river at the City of Faith and anointed hundreds of people to bestow a blessing on them. This brand of "magic" is the same as giving people a plastic horseshoe or a rabbit's foot to obtain a blessing. Using water to anoint those pitiful people and telling the story of Naaman sanction the events in the eyes of the gullible subjects.

Naaman dipped seven times in water for his leprosy, but Scripture does not instruct us to do the same. We are told to lay hands on the sick. The Bible does not sanction anointing with water in praying for the sick. This type of divination is in absolute contradiction to the Word of God. Yet, this is accepted as a gift of the Holy Spirit by many of God's people.

Dreams are used to divine. I think of the German prince who had a dream of rats. He dreamed he saw three rats: one fat, another lean, and a third blind. He sent for a learned Bohemian gypsy to interpret the dream. "The fat rat," she answered, "is your prime minister; the lean rat is your people; and the blind rat is yourself." This says it for any and all who depend on any witchcraft for personal guidance.

CLAIRVOYANCE (remote viewing) is the ability to detect physical disabilities apart from normal medical means. It is the ability to see an event or object by means other than eyesight. The authoritative quarterly *Journal of Parapsychology* calls it "extrasensory perception of objects or objective events." Clairvoyance differs from telepathy in that it seems to work without another person's mind acting as an intermediary.

Until recently most church leaders classified clairvoyance, psychoanalysis, out-of-body experiences, and other psychic phenomena as occultic. However, this attitude is changing rapidly. Morton Kelsey, a prominent Episcopal priest who teaches at Notre Dame University, came out openly in 1977 in favor of cultivating psychic experiences. In his book, *The Christian And The Supernatural*, Kelsey described Jesus as comparable to a Shaman (Psychic). He encouraged Christians to develop psychic powers such as clairvoyance, precognition and telepathy. Kelsey believes that there are some dangers in ESP, but it would help to validate the miracles claimed in the Bible.

Some clairvoyants set forth the idea that they see inside the body, as if they were looking at an X-Ray, autoscopy, as it is called. Still others simply lay hands on patients and make sweeping movements over the patients body. They disclose that from their concentration, they receive immediate diagnoses.

Clairvoyants' diagnoses range from 30% to 65% accurate.
Those said to be in direct contact with the spirit world have a higher degree of accuracy.

It is true, many prophecies of so called healers are accurate. However, any novice can make factual statements based on percentage and probability factors. It may appear there is a "clairvoyance," but in actuality the bottom line is human prophecy. The statement happens to hit THE BULL'S-EYE.

The occult power know as "clairentience" Kurt Kotch says is, "Hyperaesthesice which is an irrational (not always correct) diagnosis of illness." *(Christian Counselling & Occultism*, by Kurt Kotch, page 72-D)

The disciples asked Jesus, "What will be the sign of Your coming?"

The first words of His reply were, "Watch out that no one deceives you."

He went on to explain that His second coming would be preceded by a period of religious revival. This revival, Jesus said, would be characterized by great deception.

Psychometrics is the "Divination of facts concerning an object or its owner through contact with or proximity to the object."

A pastor friend related a story involving his mother, their neighborhood church, and himself. They were asked to write down their name and place it in the offering plate. During the meeting, the leader would give readings about the people who had written on the paper. He would give stimulating information about those in the meeting. No doubt some of the naive people thought they were observing the gift of "the Word of knowledge." In reality it was the occultic power of psychometrics, or nothing more than statements of probability. How many ministries, if examined, would prove to be mystic or occultic in nature?

Kurt Kotch studied the evils and the effects of occultism for thirty years. He concluded that possibly 95% of all fortune-telling can be regarded fake and money-making. The last 5% would then depend on extrasensory powers. Fortune-telling, demon-possessed mediums, and all forms of divination should be avoided because of their suggestive character.

"I have discovered that this ability occurs in families whose forefathers have practiced occultism and in particular magic charming. In the same way we find the New Testament talking about charismata, or 'gifts of the Holy Spirit' (I Cor. 12:9-10) 'so too, as it were, the Charismata of the devil.' " *(The Devils Alphabet*, by Kurt Kotch, page 78)

44

The name William Branham is known to most of the pentecostal community. He is unique among this group because he was a preacher of the Gospel. William Branham died in an automobile wreck. Not long before his death, he toured the pentecostal churches as a FAITH HEALER.

"William Branham, was an uneducated, timid, and poorest of the poor Baptist evangelist who in 1933, at the age of twenty-four, began to preach in Jefferson, Indiana, where over 3,000 people came to his meetings each night. It is reported that when he would meet a person he had never seen, he would be able to immediately call him by name." (Harrell, *All Things Are Possible*, page 38)

"A strange sign about Branham, (some later believed him to be more spiritualistic than spiritual) he had 'vibrations' in his left hand. When the afflicting spirit would come in contact with the gift, it set up such a physical commotion that it became visible...and so real it would stop his wrist watch instantly...like taking a live wire with too much current in it. After the oppressing spirit is cast out in Jesus' name, his red and swollen hand returns to its normal condition." (Bosworth, *Voice Of Healing*, March, 1950, page 10)

The "calling a person by name" may convince some that a "gift of knowledge" is in operation. Some may think the "red swollen hand" to be a spiritual gift. However, calling a person by name clairvoyantly is done by many psychics. The boy in India who speaks and heals in the name of Buddah also has a swelling hand to heal.

When the Holy Spirit distributes a gift of healing to one sick, it is not a result of "a method taught on how to heal." It is a "gift."

Recently I read in an ad selling a book on healing that the "supernatural can be taught." Not so, if it is of God.

Some psychic diagnoses require help from a supernatural source. However, fifty to eighty percent of illnesses are psychosomatic. The placebo effect alone cures a large number of patients. A disease produced by the mind (e.g. headache, ulcer, etc.) can be healed by the power of suggestion.

The spirit of error is born out of that which is unscrip-

tural. Jesus said, "Ye do err, not knowing the scriptures..."
(Matthew 22:29) (KJV)

The "Prosperity Philosophy," "Visualization," "Possibility Thinking," and the "God Told Me To Tell You" syndrome is "error." The reason is that they are unscriptural gimmicks concocted by man. The mind sciences depend on man rather than the Word of God. A Christian draws near to God for His blessings and healing as we do Salvation --- by Grace!

The test of any practice or doctrine must line up with the written Word.

The Shakers' doctrine was brought to this country from England by Ann Lee in 1774. The sect had its beginning in a Quaker revival in England. Its followers were called Shakers because of their ritualistic tremblings. Their shaking denoted inner conflict with the devil. They also expected the millennium momentarily and saw no need of marriage.

A firm conviction of the Shakers (some called the Shaking Quakers) was that the Spirit of Christ would again appear on earth. But this time it would be through a woman.

With this expectation firmly established, they eagerly awaited its fulfillment. They believed they had found the fulfillment complete in the personality of Ann Lee. She had united herself with the society in 1758.

Ann Lee kept busy in watchings, fastings, fears, and incessant cries to God. She labored day and night for deliverance from the very nature of sin. She suffered under the most severe tribulations and buffetings of the enemy. She was often in such extreme agony that she perspired blood through the pores of her skin.

Followers were convinced that Ann's spiritual nature exceeded any other up to that time.

During these years of spiritual experiences, her intuitive faculties grew. She studied human nature in all its phases with close attention. She developed the faculty of reading the thoughts of others. She was so unerring that she caused consternation and fear. Tales of her miraculous insight and her soul-stirring visions were voiced abroad. She became the subject of much inquiry.

Her followers became overpowered with exaltation and soon acknowledged Ann Lee as the divine Mother. They asserted that now, through woman, the second coming of Christ was fulfilled. After this she was known as Mother Ann Lee. Her followers looked to her for spiritual guidance, and her word became law. She affirmed, "I am Ann, the Word."

The laws of psychology can account for much of Mother Ann's ministration. Her followers accepted the manifestation as supernatural.

In 1800-1802 during the "Kentucky Revival," the Shakers experienced extraordinary manifestations. People walking in the streets were suddenly thrown to the ground by some unseen force. They would remain unconscious for hours. Others, without warning, would run on all fours simulating the actions of a mad dog. Even the children would shake and scream with terror.

Various unique gifts were exercised among the Shakers. There were the gifts of "pick up mother and father Joseph's crumbs." To shake and clap their hands were lively gifts. The purpose of the shaking was to shake out that which was wrong that they might inherit the Kingdom of Heaven.

The Shakers were unscriptural in many areas of their teachings including the Millennium, gifts, shaking, falling, revelations for new gifts, uncontrolled worship, Mother Ann's thought reading, and intuitive faculties mis-applied, etc. These were erroneous because the practices were not scriptural.

Fanaticism is varied. There are degrees of error in worship and in doctrine.

A manifestation that continues into this modern day is that of "falling in the spirit." In many cases the victim does not even have to be touched; it is often suggested by a slight push of the healer's hand. In some cases the suggestion is made in the presentation (sermon) before the prayer line is formed, and the suggestible fall when a hand is waved at them. A slight pressure of the healer' s hand on the subject's forehead is all it takes for the suggestible -- - down they go.

The *Associated Press* carried an article

"FAMILY SEEKS 5 MILLION FROM EVAN-GELIST - An evangelist preaching at a local church allowed an elderly woman to anguish in pain. She fell when apparently struck on the forehead and pronounced 'Slain in the Spirit.' The evangelist was Benny Hinn of Orlando, Florida. The woman was Ella Peppard, 85. She fell in the church service at Faith Tabernacle, Oklahoma, City. The lawsuit alleges Hinn 'in a deliberate and deceitful attempt to give the impression that one had been slain in the spirit,' pushed the gentleman in front of Mrs. Peppard; he fell backwards causing Mrs. Peppard to fall to the ground and break her hip.

"Hughes said Hinn declared Mrs. Peppard was hindering the service and ordered her removed from the stage. They placed her in a seat near the front of the church. He said Mrs. Peppard's family was told by witnesses that when one usher offered to seek medical aid, Hinn stopped him saying, 'Leave her alone God will heal her.' The lawsuit seeks 2.5 million in actual damages and another 2.5 million in punitive damages from Hinn Ministries, Inc. and the Faith Tabernacle (Assembly of God) Association, Inc."

The term used in the news article, "slain in the spirit," is not a New or Old Testament term. To "strike" someone on the forehead standing in a prayer line is unscriptural, as well as unwise. To fall down under these circumstances is not found in the Bible. To practice this undiscerning, hypnotic sensation is "error." What is "error?"

There is a difference between "Error," "Schism," and "Heresy," but they are all moving in the same direction.

ERROR: when one holds a wrong opinion, alone.

SCHISM: when many are brought into the error. It is the same faith; heresy makes another faith.

HERESY: Offends, separates, and rages with arguments of steel.

Practices, doctrines, and activities, not sanctioned by the Written Word of God, are examples of "error." Unchecked error will run into schism, and schism into heresy.

Our dirty laundry is rolled up into a little T.V. spot and served to us on the 6 o'clock news. The tragedy is that we Christians buy everything that is said hook, line, and sinker. The thought is projected, and the facts are edited, slanted, and colored by biased reporters. So our minds feed on distorted and incomplete facts.

When we read the papers telling us that Jimmy Swaggart is a porn addict or see a horrible picture of Jim and Tammy in the *National Enquirer*, it is natural to draw mind-shutting conclusions.

It is true that media revelations are earthly, and the Bible, not the T.V., is where we find truth. But to shut our eyes to the obvious chicanery of these frauds that are seen and heard over the television and in prayer groups is unreasonable. It is not the media that lets out the bad news. The truth is revealed when the "God told me to tell you's" open their mouths. A small amount of discernment recognizes these "God Told Me To Tell You" gimmicks. Most people have drawn their own conclusions from what they see and hear. The Scripture admonishes us to "Prove all things; hold fast that which is good." (I Thess. 5:21) (KJV)

4

MIS-DIAGNOSING

Dr. Michael Quinn, a professor at Brigham Young University, says he based his testimony not on facts, but "The Burning In The Bosom." The Mormon Church has made over 100,000 changes in their literature: The Book of Mormon, The Doctrines and Covenants, The Pearl of Great Price, and The Mormon Church History.

Changes made in the documents written by man is not important, for man's words are not infallible. The Mormons are criticized for adding to the Bible. However, many Christians today are in the same "error" in their extra-biblical revelations. The results are the same: because of some burning in the heart, head, or hand, many claim the experience is from God, ignoring Bible doctrine and warnings.

When a finance chairman makes a decision based on incomplete or inaccurate information, the result will be financial confusion. You will need an attorney to bail you out! If a surgeon performs surgery based on incomplete information, a patient may die. Religion, based on inaccurate and incomplete information, can cause a person to end up with a group in another Jonestown drinking "Kool-aid"!

There is so much going on in religion that has caused many to become confused and bewildered. Sufferance is needed from the balanced Christian when the religious super salesmen parade their fake, "God Told Me To Tell You." All one can do for a rebuttal is say, "I don't believe you," and with just as much cognition, one can say, "God told me you do not know what you are talking about." False doctrine is disproved only with the written Word of God. God does talk to His people. "My sheep recognize my voice..." (John 10:27) (LB)

The following headlines of a national magazine were no doubt written for financial remuneration. The deceptive headline read, "Bible healers who can add years to your life are curing thousands of Americans of diseases and crippling handicaps."

Those who believe such statements would have been prospects for the snake oil merchants.

The definition of "DIAGNOSING" is "to differentiate, to distinguish, to designate. It is to recognize, to have knowledge of, or to come to an understanding."

A diagnosis and prognosis from so-called healers and even legitimate medical doctors may give patients confidence. A degree of mastery, is gained over physical condition's through faith in something or someone.

Diagnosis can give a strong incentive to the patient, especially if he believes the word is direct from God.

L.A. Larue, chairman of the Committee for the Scientific Examination of Religion, has exposed some in the Faith Healing ministry as fakes. He says, "What has disappointed me is that mainline churches haven't got involved in pointing out the deception that's involved here."

Larue is a professor emeritus of Archaeology and Biblical Studies at the University of California.

Larue's statement is timely: "Why have we waited for the humanist organizations to bring this deception to the forefront?"

52

It took the murder of U.S. Congressman Leo Ryan to bring to light the terrible operation of the fraudulent Jim Jones. That neglect caused the mass murder/suicides of nearly 1,000 people on November 12, 1978.

The magician says, "You can fool part of the people all of the time and all of the people some of the time, and that is sufficient."

What a tragedy, when the ministry drops to the level of the magicians!

In light of the MIS-application of the "word of knowledge," the words of Paul in II Corinthians 4:1, 2 are appropriate here, "Therefore seeing we have this ministry, as we have received mercy, we faint not; but have renounced the hidden things of dishonesty, not walking in craftiness, nor handling the word of God deceitfully; but by manifestation of the truth commending ourselves to every man's conscience in the sight of God." (KJV)

Dishonesty in the Gospel ministry is a more nasty blow than in the secular world. The Living Bible says in II Corinthians 4:2, "We do not try to trick people into believing - we are not interested in fooling anyone. We never try to get anyone to believe that the Bible teaches what it doesn't. All such shameful methods we forego..."

What takes place when any preacher, shaman, or psychic takes upon himself to diagnose symptoms of a disease? The fake healer walks up and down the isles of an auditorium packed with the sick, crippled, and dying. He suddenly calls out someone's name. The evangelist quickly makes his or her way to that person and identifies the affliction. He also gives the subject's address and in some instances gives the doctor's name, etc. In the middle of this hype, the healer proclaims the person healed in the name of Jesus. They are faithful to point out (most of the time) that Jesus is the healer. They proclaim that the evangelist had never met the person being diagnosed or prayed for. Their proclamation is that legs are lengthened, teeth are filled, spinal columns are reconstructed, and cancer dies in their presence.

This method of diagnosis has a low rate of accuracy.

Years ago only 50% of diagnoses by the medical profession were accurate. And even now with modern technology diagnosis is not even close to 100% accurate. Often alternate diagnostic possibilities are given to the patient.

The Gospel ministry is stepping out of their bounds to diagnose diseases and symptoms! Diagnosis that is as accurate as possible is needed to write a prescription for medical cure. The medical profession needs accurate diagnosis because a prognosis is needed. The purpose for a medical prognosis is to obtain a cure. Diagnosis by a "healer" is ridiculous. The expressed purpose of the "healer" is to bring health to that person, not to tell him what his disease is. A diagnosis need not come into the picture. If medical doctors could "heal," they would never have to diagnose or write a prescription.

The bone of contention is that to diagnose illnesses is serious. The healer surmises, "God is revealing to me a certain sickness or symptom." In the name of common sense, though, why would God want to do such a thing? Diagnosing without a certificate is illegal. Section 2141 of the Laws Relating to the Practice of Medicine and Surgery reads:

> "Any person, who practices or attempts to practice, or who advertises or holds himself out as practicing, any system or mode of treating the sick or afflicted or who diagnoses, treats, operates for, or prescribes for any ailment, blemish, deformity, disease, disfigurement, disorder, injury, or other mental or physical condition of any person, without having at the time or so doing a valid, unrevoked certificate... is guilty of a misdemeanor."

This section 2141 would put every healing minister and psychic healer into jail. Happily, those who do not wish to close the doors to legitimate healing ministries in line with the Word of God have added ameliorative section 2146. It reads: "Nothing in this (section) shall be construed so as to discriminate against any particular school of medicine or surgery, or any other treatment, nor shall it regulate, treatment, nor shall it regulate, prohibit or apply any kind of treatment by prayer, nor interfere in any way with the practice of religion.''

There seems to be a mutually contradictory character of the above two sections; however, ''Any person who...advertises or holds himself out as practicing any system...of treating the sick...'' means just that. We can see these two sections point out the paradoxical nature of the spiritual versus the medical healing controversy.

It is true the ''healer'' does not perform surgery. However, the reason section 2141 law was written is to protect the public. Those who put trust in fraudulent practitioners who give false diagnoses place themselves in potential danger. When a person is prayed for and proclaimed healed, the patient often discards his life-sustaining medicine. As a result, the patient trusting in the bogus diagnosis could be in danger. *The ministry should not attempt to diagnose illness, and the practice is not sanctioned by the written Word of God.*

A woman entered a police station and confessed that she had shot and killed her son. Why? She did it because an astrologer predicted her ill son would never regain mental health. To save her son from a horrible future, she killed him. The astrologer, like many healers, went free, but not the mother! The healer can proclaim one healed, and the same tragedy (death) could be the result.

Richard Roberts calls out diseases during his T.V. program. While talking with his guests, he will say something like this, ''O.K. Lord, yes...uh-huh, yes Lord...O.K. I will do that. All right. I will...''

When he gets a break from talking with his guests (puts God on hold), he gives HIS ''word of knowledge.'' He continues, ''The Lord was just giving me a word of knowledge. Someone...I want to say growth. I see a boil. It is right down on the left leg...Its about an inch in diameter...The Lord is healing the boil right now. You are looking at the boil now, wondering if it's you I am talking about.''

His so-called word of knowledge is an irrational diagnosis, but it is a diagnosis. It is unsound because God has nothing to do with it. He said it was a boil and stated the size of the inflamed area where it was located. This self-appointed prophet threw in a little extra information and said the person being diagnosed was "looking at the boil." He said someone in television land was wondering if he really was the one being diagnosed. This, if true, would have been an incredible revelation that involved more than a physical diagnosis. No doctor, psychic, prophet, apostle (including Paul) has ever boasted of this all-inclusive style of remote viewing type of "diagnosing," erroneously called "a word of knowledge."

He continues, "I can see the boil on the left leg, and the size is about an inch in diameter!" If he really did view a boil and the size, it would have to be the occultic power of clairvoyance. It authoritatively is not the Word of Knowledge of I Corinthians 12:8. The key word is "if."

One might wonder if this could be mind reading. Mind reading requires the sender and the receiver of thoughts to be in contact through concentration. Mind reading could not work many times under these circumstances because T.V. programs are often delayed before they are aired, sometimes for weeks. Most of the bogus "word of knowledge" is stated on T.V. film and aired at a later date. When the T.V. program is viewed, the Healer Evangelist could be off fishing, sleeping, or dead. Mind reading could not be the issue. At any rate, MIND READING is not their claim. For certain, the "art" of mind reading is not "a Word of Knowledge." (I Cor. 12:8)

In my reclining chair, (survey), of several ministries that use this incredible type of diagnosing, I have heard approximately only twenty-five diseases called out. This is the combined number of all the T.V. evangelists. The Medical Encyclopedia states there are over six hundred symptoms of man's diseases. The obvious question is, why are so few of the six hundred symptoms called out so the sick can be healed? Surely, there are many others in

T.V. land who would like to be healed! And surely, God would love to heal them.

Credit can be given to John Wimber for some imagination in this area of diagnosing. During the time of "calling out" their so called "word of knowledge" on the 700 Club, with Pat Robertson and others, Wimber gave his special word. There was out in T.V. land a new born baby born with both male and female sexual organs. "Just go over and pray for the baby, and one of those sexual organs will disappear."

How spell-binding it would be to hear the disease of Cholangitis, a serious infection, or Proctitis, Pterygium, Exophthalmos, Dacryocystitis, Xanthelasma, Blepharitis, and Addisons disease (an Adrenal Insufficiency). People with these diseases would appreciate their symptoms being called out at least once in a while so they could also be "healed."

It is strange that a God who cares about backaches and sinus passes up those with Exophthalmos and Xanthelasma. He knows the number of the hairs on our head, and notices when the sparrow falls. But this same God forgets to remind the modern day prophet to call out Dacryocystitis? Amazing! Do you suppose God isn't "familiar" with these symptoms?

A safeguard for the "healer" is that a few people are helped because they have a psychosomatic illness. When the healer diagnoses a serious illness such as terminal cancer, who can prove or disprove the diagnosis? Genuine healings and miracles can be authenticated only with a medical diagnosis before and after the alleged healing!

Seventy percent of America has some form of back trouble. A T.V. evangelist's audience of 10,000,000 means seven million people have lumbago in some form. A back diagnosis is a sure-fire hit for the T.V. diagnostician.

Jim Jones protected himself from fraud with the following statement in the People's Forum, April 1976, which reads, "As it is understood that only a medical physician or psychiatrist can determine accurately whether the source of the physical problems are psychological or psychosomatic, there is no attempt to say what the physical problem could be.''

Jim Jones took proper legal steps to protect himself. Trusted aides provided information about who was in the audience with various pains, stomach aches, and the like. However, when he missed predictions, he was protected by this statement in the forum, ''There is no attempt to say what the physical problems could be.''

Here is the admission by Jim Jones, for he knew his diagnosing was fraud. Charismatic fortune-tellers call out more than just physical needs. They include prophecies concerning jobs, marriage matching, professions, moral conduct, finances, and etc.

There is something in the structure of man that reaches out for the para-normal experience.

A cemetery in Jedda, Arabia was visited annually by thousands of Mohammedans. They dropped money in a slot, asked for and received Eve's advice through a speaking tube. This alleged mausoleum was destroyed in 1927. The woman who had run the racket from an underground room retired with a fortune. She was not the last person to exploit others with the "unknown."

An evangelist, who traveled for years across America, tells of an experience that is blatantly irreverent. This preacher worked with a Polly Parrot in church services. The parrot would garble out syllables, supposedly representing glossolalia (tongues). One of the members would give an interpretation. Such incredulous occurrences are embarrassing to the body of Christ.

The gullible will always be easy prey to religious fakes. However, Fundamental Bible believers, balanced pentecostals, humanist, or saint can discern a gimmick. Gimmicks do not impress the thinking public. Religious fakery is spotlighted in Ezekial 13:1-3, "And the word of the Lord came unto me [Ezekial], saying, Son of man, prophesy against the prophets of Israel that prophesy, and say thou unto them that prophesy *out of their own hearts*, Hear ye the word of the Lord; Thus saith the Lord

God; Woe unto the foolish prophets, *that follow their own spirit, and have seen nothing!*" (KJV)

There are certain tools of the psychic trade used by all "diagnosticians." Some T.V. and other evangelists qualify; however, their technique and results are of bargain basement quality. Their kind of prophecy is like saying, "The stock market will go up, then down, then up, then down. There will be babies born in India, a jet liner with three hundred aboard will arrive late at Kennedy Airport. No cure will be discovered for high doctors' fees. During dry weather days, some farm states will have dust. Things will become more expensive."

These type of prophecies are of no more value than a Chinese fortune cookie or the daily astrological forecasts.

Religious fortune-telling operates in the same "fenced in area" of all other psychics. Their prophecies boil down to a vague mass of garbled statements.

The crystal ball gazer had just collected her large fee for a reading and told the visitor, "This entitles you to ask me two questions."

"Isn't that a lot of money for only two questions?" the startled visitor asked!

"Yes, it is," answered the fortune-teller. "And now what is your second question?"

When irrational diagnosis is put to the test, the results of the claim are inescapable...IT JUST AIN'T LIKE THEY ARE SAYING IT! When a religious fortune-teller does go out on a limb and states times, dates, addresses, and etc. then their miscalculations become visible.

Another man who operates out of St. Louis, Missouri boldly presents his pre-digested information to his congregation. He stores his information on small slips of paper inserted in his Bible. He's not at all shy about telling his followers that he speaks directly with God as he stands before them in person. He stands there listening as the Divinity speaks to him apparently giving the name, address, and ailments of the subject.

In Stockton, California it appeared that God told him

about a bearded man sitting on the aisle. The evangelist called him by name. He assured the audience he had never spoken to this man before and proceeded to describe the man's problems. And he declared these problems solved. The unfortunate chap thereupon fell to the floor and appeared to be in the throes of either ecstasy or death.

The man agreed. The evangelist groped about and then divined that Tom had serious mental and drinking problems and again obtained agreement from him. Then the preacher put his hand on Tom's head and gave the desired information. "Some people have condemned you because of your financial status...the only way I can know about you is if God speaks to me; God says He will heal you."

The evangelist's wife gave him that information. The man he called out was a bachelor. He didn't drink; he had a secure federal job and was not named Tom. When the evangelist's wife had approached him earlier in the evening to strike up a conversation, he'd given her that false information.

Tom's real name is Don Henvick and is a member of the Society of American Magicians.

Personal prophecies, cure rate, and claims by self-appointed prophets always sounds better than they are. We must keep in mind when considering results that approximately 80% of the people who are sick in America will get well anyway. The psychic preachers rely upon these statistics.

Faith healers dread straight rational scientific evaluation of their claims. For that which is so popular and so practiced, faith healing has a remarkably undocumented success rate. The reason is "before and after" medical examination is absolutely essential. This is not often available.

In 1955 Oral Roberts was offered $1,000 for evidence of any cures by the Church of Christ. Roberts offered to the press two of the "most striking instances of cures" he could muster.

One of the two had never obtained a diagnosis from a physician and the other later underwent orthodox surgery to remove the tumor that had been "healed and removed."

One of the tactics of Jim Jones's operation was supposedly diagnosing illnesses. Early in his ministry Jones learned methodology by attending sessions of other "faith healers." Jones knew every trick of the trade, and he used them all.

Jones's spies obtained personal information about people.

Then Jones would point out those people in the church services and bring out the "revelations" he saw about them. Temple members who worked in the post office, in hospitals, and other places supplied information to Jones upon request. One woman tells the story of how a Temple member visited her the day before a meeting to which she was invited. Jones had a revelation about her at the meeting. The pattern was repeated several times before she learned how they were gaining access to private information.

Jones carried this bogus "revelation" knowledge farther than the typical religious diagnostician. He kept some people in bondage by the claim that he knew everything they said and did.

Jones's members tell of the night he singled out a particular woman and said, "You lied to me; drop dead."

And she fell to the floor. In the back of the room a man rose and said, "I don't believe that. It's a fake."

Jones said, "You drop dead."

That man also dropped to the floor. But before the evening was over, Jones brought them "back to life." Each in turn knelt before him, thanking him objectively for his grace.

Rumors got around that Jones had resurrected more than forty people from the dead. Jim Jones was a modern day Simon Magnus. "Beloved, believe not every spirit, but try the spirits whether they are of God: because many false prophets are gone out into the world." (I John 4:1) (KJV)

In the book *Beyond Seduction*, author Dave Hunt tells of a major healing ministry in the Los Angeles area:

"One Saturday evening in a crusade that had those attending applauding the Lord with joyful fervor, 'miraculous healings' were reported. What a time it was for strengthening one's faith! And what a disillusioning experience for the young man who as part of his ministry, followed up these 'miracles' over the next two weeks. Instead of the testimonies he expected to obtain, he discovered that not one of the eighty had actually been healed! Yet many of them had sincerely testified to healings that evening in front of 1,000's. They were deceived into an apparent temporary psychosomatic loss of symptoms by the mass enthusiasm."

This shot-gun type of diagnosing is sure-fire. Any one can manage a healing service in this manner.

At times the media has seriously tried to investigate faith healing results. Back in April 1956, *The Fresno* (California) *Bee* surveyed those who had been prayed for by A.A. Allen in a three-week revival there. They covered some four hundred miles, interviewing everyone they could.

They found that some of the claimed illnesses were entirely imaginary in the first place and had been self-diagnosed.

Those who had permitted Allen to quote their case as a testimony confessed their illness had never been declared cured. One Colorado victim had traveled over one thousand miles to get treatment from the evangelist. He had been declared cured of liver cancer and had returned home only to die of the disease two weeks later.

I absolutely believe God heals people today as He did in Bible days and is a miracle-working, prayer-answering God! In our church services we pray for the sick every Sunday. However, what I have or have not personally witnessed with my physical eyes has nothing to do with the truth of God's Word. Those of us who believe in miracles know anything is possible with God. Yet we must admit we have never witnessed some of the things "proclaimed" by others. When unusual miracles are proclaimed before thousands such as a crooked leg, etc., who is game to go up to the platform and ask to see the proof?

There is a story about a husband that despised his wife's cat. The cat was always under his feet, leaving scratch marks on the furniture, and shedding hair on his trousers.

While his wife was visiting her mother one week, the man took the cat and drowned it. His wife was in hysterics when she returned to find her cat gone. To comfort her, the husband made the grand gesture of taking out an ad in the newspapers and offering $1,000 for the cat's safe return. A friend hearing about the man's offer and not knowing the details, said, "Man, you're crazy. That's a huge reward to offer for a cat."

The man smiled and replied, "When you know what I know, you can afford to take the risk."

Many of the "healer's" tactics and declarations just can't be proved. Since they know what they know, their odds are better than the house at Las Vegas.

A member of the church I now pastor was the funeral director in charge of Wesley Parker's funeral. Wesley, age 11, died as a result of his parents' withholding his insulin. Funeral director, Wes Dixon, provided me with the book, *We Let Our Son Die*:

> Snapping off the rubber band that held the newspaper in a folded position, I opened it to expose the front page. A small head line at the bottom caught my eye: PARKERS HELD TO ANSWER IN 'FAITH' DEATH'. I glanced at the title and sat down in a chair next to the table lamp to read.
>
> Barstow--Lawrence and Alice Parker were held to answer criminal charges yesterday in the faith healing death of their 11 year old diabetic son, Wesley.
>
> The Parkers are accused of withholding the insulin treatment for their son's diabetes from August 19 to August 22 when the boy died. The Parkers previously said they believed their son had been healed by a visiting minister at their church August 19 and Wesley would be resurrected.'
>
> The Parkers believed their son had been healed

by a visiting minister. In effect the preacher 'DIAGNOSED' the diabetic boy as being healed of diabetes. They were so sure of the 'DIAGNOSIS,' they even had a birthday party for the deceased Wesley, expecting him to walk in the door and were crushed when he didn't.

The local news paper release reads; "Barstow-- Wesley Parker age 11, is buried in Mountain View Cemetery. Mountain View Cemetery is on the other side of town. It is a hopeful place, a verdant square planted with trees. The green ends at the fence line, where the daily irrigation gives way to the Mojave's pine and grayish brown colored rock shimmering into the distance. The cemetery says a lot about Barstow, an optimistic town strung along route 66 and the Sante Fe Railroad, where 18,000 residents hope that a nation of travelers will stop long enough to buy some gas, food, or a nights rest. After three days without insulin, Wesley Parker died. His father and mother, faith unshaken and Bibles clutched to their hearts, arranged for special services in a local funeral parlor where they predicted, God would raise Wesley from the dead and send him out to walk among men and teach the glory of the Word. The Parkers took their shoes off (Holy ground) and commanded Wesley to rise from the dead, in Jesus' name. They did this because they were confident their son would be resurrected. This was witnessed by Wes Dixon, the funeral director. Wesley did not rise. On the following morning the undertaker, following direction from Wesley's father, took the body to the cemetery and in the company of a grave digger and the cemetery manager, committed Wesley Parker to the ground without a prayer...An officer stood before the father of Wesley and said, 'Mr. Parker, we've investigated your son's death, and have come to place you and your wife under arrest.' The officer looked at a small card in his hand and began to read; 'You have the absolute right to remain silent. Anything you say can and will be used against you in a court of law...''

(Information from the book, *We Let our Son Die - A Parent's Search For Truth*, by Larry Parker as told to Don

Tanner. Harvest House Publishers, Irvine, CA)

The great faith preacher who "diagnosed" young Wesley as healed contributed to his faith-murder. This is the reason for section 2141 of the laws relating to the practice of medicine and surgery. "DIAGNOSING" by preachers should be prohibited by law.

Man is not capable of "reading another person's mail." The following quote was written a long time ago, but it relates to what is happening in our time: "As he is traitor to his Prince who taketh upon him to coin moneys out of a base metal, yea although in the stamp he putteth forth, show the image of the Prince, so he that shall broach doctrine that cometh not from God, whatsoever He set on it, is a traitor unto God; yea in truth, a cursed traitor, though he was an angel from heaven." (Abbot 1562-1635)

Another old but "current" truth is "Error is never so likely to do mischief, as when it comes to us under the pretension and patronage of that which is true." (Cumming)

The following interview was on the Johnny Carson Show:

CARSON: Your latest thing. You've been working on faith healers?

RANDI: I've investigated quite a number of them over the years, but the three I've concentrated on lately, one W.V. Grant, David Paul, and a man named Peter Popoff. W.V. Grant does not use anything very original. He tells people to leap out of the wheel chairs and run around them. He carries thirty wheel chairs with him in a huge van. They know they can walk but the audience at home watching the T.V. program thinks they cannot walk, but they come into the building with perhaps a cane. The wheel chairs are provided for their convenience. Now this is Flim-Flam; there is no question about it.

CARSON: Is everything phony? Is it possible that one might rise from the wheel chair?

RANDI: Oh, they certainly can, but people like

W.V. Grant for example, they research the audience very carefully. They see somebody walking in and getting out of the wheelchair and edging along to the seat. They know that person is actually mobile. But someone with the electric wheel chair for example, they don't get anywhere near that person. They know that person can't literally walk, and they won't take a chance on it. Grant has other techniques, too, that are very common; for example, he sends his wife and some of his ministers in advance and gets the information from the people. Then he calls them out by means of divine inspiration. He is supposed to have the anointed gift of the Spirit whereby he can call people by name and name their illness because God speaks directly to him.

CARSON: That sounds like Joe Dunninger. You're not saying that faith does not serve a useful purpose?

RANDI: Oh, it does. Psychosomatic diseases can be relieved this way, and unfortunately we sometimes take away the symptoms and we don't take away the disease, and that can be very dangerous. It's like popping pills. You take away the pain and the disease is still there, and that can't help you.

CARSON: You have a tape (video) here. Can you tell us what we're going to see, and how you did this, and what it will show?

RANDI: We researched Peter Popoff very well, and Rev. Popoff is not going to be very happy with us, I don't think. You are going to see a segment tape as if you are watching it at home. You will apparently see a healing. We went to Houston, Texas and discovered - of all things - the man was wearing a hearing aid in his left ear. A man who heals the deaf and blind isn't going to have much need for a hearing aid, I don't think. At the meeting in San Francisco, we used Alex Jason, an expert in electronics, and a surveillance man, and we picked up something interesting.

(Note: The segment was played on the Carson show, revealing only what the audience saw. Then it was replayed with the Flim-Flam added in.)

CARSON: These two people (subjects being prayed for) had not met Popoff?

RANDI: That's right. Popoff had never spoken to the couple being prayed for.

CARSON: Yet Popoff calls the man's name and house number?

RANDI: He calls out the people's address, and the people were astonished to hear this because they did not tell him. But what was not known is that Popoff's wife had been touring around the audience getting into conversations, "Is Jesus going to heal you today? I see, where do you live?" And they have filled out healing cards in advance to the program and handed them in. And now back stage someone is sitting at a transmitter. Here is the segment of Popoff praying with these two people.

(Note: The bold type is the voice of the evangelist's wife transmitted from behind the stage, feeding information to the evangelist, a supposed WORD OF KNOWLEDGE.)

(Popoff walks near the couple he is to deal with.)

Jerry Reed.

Popoff: Is it Jerry Reed?

Its a woman. She's praying for her husband, Harold.

Popoff: Who is Harold?

He's got cataracts.

Popoff: I just believe that God is going to burn those cataracts off your eyes, right now.

He lives at 34788 Foothill Drive.

Popoff: 34788 Foothill Drive? I'll tell you the angels of God are round about your home; just take those glasses off..."

(Popoff turns from talking to the man and directs his attention to the woman standing by the man)

67

She's got eye problems too!

Popoff: You've got glaucoma. I want you to put your hands over your eyes as I pray...Sister, you've got eye problems, too. Take your glasses off, lay your hands over your eyes. (Here it comes, God is going to give these precious ones divine surgery.) Right now, Jesus!

(End of dialogue transmitted by electronics.)

CARSON: That's disturbing when you see it. You tend to laugh at it, yet these people are obviously so impressed with what's going on.

RANDI: Oh! They are absolutely impressed. You see the people collapse and fall to the floor. Tears running down their faces, believe their kids on drug addiction are going to be healed, now because he's talking to God, that God speaks directly to him because he's an anointed minister, and there are three things that amaze me about that first of all,

1. God's frequency (I didn't know He used radio) is 39.170 megahertz.

2. That God is a woman.

3. That God's voice sounds exactly like Popoff's wife, Elizabeth.

CARSON: Does Popoff know about this tape?

RANDI: No, he did not know about this tape until this very moment.

CARSON: There's a lot of money in this kind of business, isn't there?

RANDI: Ten to twenty million dollars a year to each one of them and remember, not one cent of tax, and all they have to do is pay tax on the $200 or so a week they take as a personal salary. The rest of it can go into the mattress or into their back pocket. Now mind you they claim they're helping people in Haiti, Ethiopia, and what not, sure they might be doing that, but I have an idea if someone really looked into it, they might find some different news there. They don't have to pay one cent of tax. They don't have to account for any of their income to anyone in the government or any other agency.

CARSON: What is the legal position on this?

RANDI: We have tried to interest the States and Federal attorney in this, and we've taken the evidence that you've just seen. We've taken much more than that. I mean really dreadful evidence to people, and they cluck and they say, "It's a pity what these people are doing to the American public." We say "What are you going to do about it?" "Ahh...well, call me Friday!" That's the end of it.

CARSON: You're talking about so-called quote "Religion" and that's very icy.

RANDI: That's right. It's a political hot potato; no one will touch it.

(End of segment.)

Could it be that some evangelists are reading thoughts? Thoughts of another person can be read by a trained mind reader. The ability to read other's thoughts is an acquired ability; it is not a supernatural gift!

Joseph Dunninger was one of the world's foremost "thought readers." He claimed 90% accuracy due to his many years of steady research. He kept $10,000 available if anyone could prove he employed paid assistants in his demonstrations. He did not tolerate those who preyed on the gullible, who claimed to see tomorrow.

He would read the names on calling cards of people he had never seen. He would tell how much money one had in his pocket. He revealed the denominations of the coins and the dates if the person held the information in his mind.

He would tell the person holding a book the number of the page and repeat the very words that person silently read.

People were amazed as he would tell the contents in a steal box or a safe. He read the thoughts of the only person who knew the contents. Joe Dunninger said, "Each and every one of us are senders of thoughts."

Dunninger's book *The Art Of Thought Reading* was printed to teach anybody how to read thoughts. He said the thought reader is no different from the accomplished pianist, the artist, and the mathematical expert. Thought reading recognizes no distance.

Thought reading is not the word of knowledge nor any other of the nine gifts of the Holy Spirit. It is knowledge picked out of the mind of a human. A word of knowledge is the knowledge of God picked out of the Bible by the Holy Spirit, applied to the heart of a person. Nothing else!!

5

WHY DO THEY GO
FOR QUACKS?

In a 1969 psychic booklet there were a number of articles about strange phenomena of our times. The Rev. Willard Fuller of Palatka, Florida was one of the people included. He claimed to insert dental fillings without the client's opening his mouth. He fixed ordinary fillings, crowns into gold, and made crooked teeth start growing straight in his clients...just by calling on Jesus to do it.

When asked what gives him the ability to cause gold to come into a tooth, Fuller explains, "Something special happened to me in 1960. A charismatic experience swept me into a completely new spiritual encounter. God gave me the gifts of healing, miracles, and the discerning of spirits. I touch people on the head or the face in prayer, and the healing occurs."

Thousands have testified to having received supernatural fillings. Fuller has hundreds of written testimonies of every description. Other manifestations of unusual nature have taken place during Fuller's ministry. Balls of fire have appeared low over the building where Fuller was praying for people. Gold sometimes spiraled in the air in front of the auditorium near the evangelist.

One question, please...concerning Willard Fuller! How is it that he not only wears thick glasses to correct his eyesight, but also has six missing teeth himself, and the rest of his teeth are badly stained and contain quite ordinary silver fillings? Physician, heal thyself!

People fall for chicanery more quickly when it's delivered before an audience of millions and especially when done in the name of Jesus.

A young man phoned into the radio talk show to Bob Larson and stated, "I do believe W.V. Grant has the power to heal. Now the person is not going to get healed, who does not believe, so I think in order for him to make up for those times that the people don't get healed, he has to have some fakery in there. But I do think he has the power to heal."

It is mind-boggling to imagine that a person with a primary knowledge of the Bible would make such a statement. It is this kind of mentality that permits fakes to operate year after year.

When a religion is wrapped in a multi-million dollar package, some think, it must be of God! Some big ministries center on nothing more than healing, prophecy, miracles, and the success philosophy. It all seems so righteous to the material-minded person!

Deception comes in convincing fashion, wearing the garb of authenticity. The gullible are duped into swallowing lies, thinking all the while they are digesting the truth. In reality they are underscoring the well-known words of Phineas Taylor Barnum, "There is a sucker born every minute."

There is a very fine line between the spiritual and the occult. This is why immature Christians are deceived.

America, evidently, has not had her fill of ripoffs and hucksters. The number seems to be growing.

Today diagnosing is practiced by Sue Wallace, known as a "Doctor of Magneto Therapy." She attempts to diagnose, while wearing a wire contraption on her head. She says her ability is in a magic wire pyramid. She deals with her victims in a one-to-one encounter. Sue Wallace has the patient stand beside her, one arm extended straight out to the side. She thinks of some part of the body and then pulls down on the arm of the sick person. If the arm goes down real easily, then there is trouble in the area Sue was thinking of. Sue's percent of hits could be only the typical.

Edgar Cayce is known as the most phenomenal psychic of all time. His 14,000 readings continue to be researched to this day. It is reported that he could absorb a subject by simply sleeping on a book.

He would give "readings" by knowing only the person's name and address. He would "diagnose" the illness and then give a prognosis, helping the sick back to health. Many people believed in Edgar Cayce to the extent that the Cayce Foundation houses his 14,000 readings. 8,976 of these readings are devoted to medical subjects. Fourteen million words were transcribed while Cayce was in a self-induced trance.

Many fell back on this sleeping prophet to prove the paranormal, who is credited with having made accurate diagnoses. However, Cayce is also remembered for his apparent successes, not his failures. Cayce - like all other diagnosticians - was fond of expressions like, "I feel that..." and "Perhaps." These qualifying words are often used to avoid positive declarations.

A percentage of the letters sent to Cayce contained specific details about illnesses. There was nothing to stop Cayce from presenting that information as if it were a divine revelation. Cayce was in many ways different from the run-of-the-mill psychics, but he used the same technique of generalization that all fortune-tellers and healers use.

People go for quacks for the same reason a river is crooked. The path of least resistance is chosen by those who think they can "get something for nothing!"

It really does not take an out-of-the-ordinary discernment to detect the charismatic fortune-telling quack. It is something like when Justice John M. Harlan once explained the intricacies of evidence to a young man. "Usually in conflicting evidence one statement is far more probable than the other, so that we can decide easily which to believe. It is like a boy and the house hunter. A house hunter getting off the train at a suburban station said to a lad, "My boy, I'm looking for Mr. Smithson's new block of semi-detached cottages. How far are they from here?"

"About twenty minute walk," the boy replied.

"Twenty minutes!" exclaimed the house hunter. "Nonsense, the advertisement says five."

"Well," said the boy, "You can believe me, or you can believe the advertisement, but I ain't trying to make a sale."

Too many people are believing advertisements!

6

DIVINE HEALING
OR MYSTICISM?

What is a "PLACEBO?"

The University of South Carolina researchers found that stress was a factor in the illnesses of 75% of the people studied in clinics. Stress was frequently involved in heart disease, backaches, diarrhea, depression, and other disorders. They said that stress can also impair the immune system's ability to function and play a role in the disease of cancer. Biofeedback, guided imagery, self-hypnosis, and progressive muscular relaxation were used by the university doctors to help fight stress.

Documented testimonials of healings and miracles attest to the fact that all religions experience the phenomenal. Just because someone gets well of a physical sickness does not necessarily constitute what some term a divine healing or miracle.

MYSTICISM believes in Deity in some degree. Mysticism is "a belief that the direct knowledge of God and truth is possible to man through an extension of his spiritual insight toward union with the substance and essence of divinity."

In common practice "mysticism" is a simple and abiding

faith in the power of God. This faith in God is to accomplish all things necessary to the life and happiness of man. This definition might satisfy some people's philosophy of the Christian faith.

The Christian's faith in Jesus Christ is not "Mysticism!" Christianity is a relationship with the person, Jesus Christ. A Christian believes in the virgin birth, life, blood, and resurrection of Jesus. Mysticism does not accept faith in Jesus Christ.

All "faith" is effective. But real and effective faith is that which is placed in Jesus Christ. Luke 8:48 recounts the story of a woman who had been subject to bleeding for twelve years. She touched the edge of Jesus' cloak, and immediately her bleeding stopped. Jesus said in verse 48, "Daughter...your faith has healed you. Go in peace." (LB)

It was her faith that brought her healing. She was not just psychologically healed. The healing was physical, and the healer was Jesus; thus, a "divine healing."

When medicine was primitive, doctors, not knowing what to do, prescribed sugar pills or colored water. There was no medicinal value, yet patients experienced relief after the medicine was applied. This form of treatment is called "the placebo effect." It has been quoted that thirty to sixty percent who receive a placebo will experience some relief. The placebo has no proven applications in itself. It works because the person taking it expects it to work. He starts thinking in terms of recovery rather than sickness. Placebo is an illusion, but since our lives are shaped by our perceptions, we may find help in a placebo.

Doctors say some people are helped psychologically by "FAITH" healing generated by healers. They can improve physically. There are many others who do not find help (especially those with a terminal illness). They become guilt-ridden when healing does not come, as faith has been taught to them.

The psychosomatic, or FAITH, or the placebo can cure certain ailments. It can be activated by a device or even by a situation. To be effective, "suggestion" must reach the hidden layers of the mind. This depends on the whole situation.

Nothing can be laid down as to what kind of personality constitutes a FAITH, SPIRITUAL HEALER. Medicine is an incomplete science, and medical doctors are sometimes puzzled by spontaneous remissions. Every method has its proportion of cures and also of relapses.

For every "real," there is a counterfeit. The devil's counterpart is possible to come out of our psychological makeup. Demon activity is especially active in some foreign countries. The ancient Greek Oracle of Delphi, at Corinth, spoke in tongues (counterfeit glossalalia). When these priests and priestesses spoke a false glossalalia, it was not the Spirit of God. It was mysticism.

Mystical healings are faith healings that depend on psychological and biological results of sincere conviction upon the functional processes of organic structures of the body.

The born again Christian is in a personal relationship with Jesus Christ. We release our FAITH in Jesus based only on God's written Word. When a divine healing from Christ takes place, it does not eliminate human chemistry, to work its wonders and renew the life of the flesh. Modern scientists are inclined to believe that the healings resulting from faith are only psychological rather than spiritual. Mystic faith does give results, but is based on a "psychological" experience only. When one is healed, according to the Scriptures, the results are SPIRITUAL, as well as PHYSICAL. A touch from Jesus includes, but is beyond, a psychological happening.

A psychological experience will not bring spiritual growth from the Lord Jesus Christ. Diseases due to hysteria or melancholy are acutely susceptible to psychological cures. However, it appears from many testimonials that FAITH (All kinds of faith) can also work healings beyond that of a psychological experience.

Dr. Paul Meir said, " I have studied the forty most common defense mechanisms by which all four billion human beings on planet earth deceive themselves daily from the truth. Through the use of suggestion, I have cured many patients of imagined illnesses such as blindness, paralysis, hypoglycemia, epilepsy, and multiple sclerosis.''

Studies of the miracles at Lourdes show that cures fall into regular patterns of healing by suggestions. However, about one case a year, admittedly, remains puzzling. Some of the shrines that heal by suggestion puzzle some hospital physicians because they report some real, spontaneous remissions.

Danny Korem, a professional magician who is a Christian has innovated over one hundred magical effects. This imaginary theory is called SSP, which stands for ''subtle sensory perception.'' He was able to accomplish many feats with this fraudulent theory. It appeared he was exercising the occult of precognition (to predict the future), telepathy, and so forth.

Korem says, ''Those who pose to have supernatural powers work on the principles of probability, psychological, as well as medical phenomena, that comes into play. Many so called DIVINE HEALERS pose to have spiritual powers. They, too, depend on the psychological and the probability factors that are on their side.''

The ancient mystics practiced the ''laying on of hands,'' as do many Christians and others. The mystic believes himself to possess a spiritual power derived from God. He believes he is able to communicate healing power by touching their heads or the affected parts of their bodies. By this contact the spiritual virtue passes into the sufferer's body. This mystical practice was not equal to the Bible's instruction to lay hands on the sick and anoint them with ''OIL.'' God's Word does not teach that healing comes from any person other than Jesus Christ. Some modern day so-called healers convey the idea that healing power is in their hands.

The power is not in the hands to heal as the mystics believe. Here again, there is only a fine line that divides the occult and the spiritual.

The reason people died in the church at Corinth (I Cor. 11:29: ''...not discerning the Lord's body.'') (KJV) was they did not recognize that healing came from the body of Jesus.

If power were resident in the hands, the Bible would affirm that fact with a statement in the Holy Scriptures. Our instruction in James 5:15 is, ''And the prayer of faith shall save the sick, and the Lord shall raise him up..." (KJV)

To insinuate there is divine healing in anybody other than Jesus or in any method other than Jesus' way is unscriptural.

The reason for "laying on of hands" is we are told to do so in the Scriptures; the reason is God's business.

The sixth day that Oral Roberts was in his Prayer Tower (March 28, 1987) in Tulsa, Oklahoma, surrounded by some of the regents, he made the following statement:

> "I have been rekindling the healing gifts of God in my life. He (God) started with me in my hand, with the power of God in my hand. There are people with me in the room, like Charles Blair, who early called me to Denver to a crusade and he saw the manifestation of God, and MY HAND IS LIKE IT IS ON FIRE AGAIN. I don't know whether to laugh or cry the way I feel...I know that we are close to victory...(to getting the $8,000,000.)"

To claim that "power" is in the hands smacks of mysticism.

It is possible that after a religious person is told that someone has a burning hand, he will believe in "that" hand. They in fact may receive a psychological healing. The "burning hand" is their placebo. Divine healing from a person's hand? No!

In mystic religions, people must have someone or something to believe in. The Christian looks to Jesus for divine healing. The white magician (Christian mystic) encourages people to look to him. He directs people to his prayers, gimmicks, plans, and visions of a burning hand rather than to Jesus Christ only.

These so-called divine healers eventually drift into using mystical and magical methods. There are so many, many people who desire God, yet in honest error place their faith in people such as the witch doctors in Africa, the shamans of Asia and America, priests and physicians of classical Greece, Oriental and popular mystics, psychics such as Edgar Cayce and Nostradamus, swamis, medicine men, T.V. evangelists, preachers, pastors, white magic preachers, fortune-tellers, doctors, psychiatrists, and many others.

People also place their faith in places, such as The Shrine of Our Lady of Fatima in Lourdes, France, church buildings, and other places considered "holy," the newest one being Medigorue in Yugoslovia. Holy testimonies indicate they have received healings, miracles, and other blessings at these places.

People can place their faith in things such as: blessing packs (with pledge books, literal mustard seeds, miracle billfolds, anointed cloths (thousands of yards that are run through a cutting machine into four and six-inch squares to be mailed in envelopes), Holy water (supposedly from the Jordan River, actually from a water tap in America), plastic gloves representing God's hand, jars of honey, miniature plastic bags filled with cement sent in envelopes for offerings, plastic bags filled with sugar, plastic bags with water from the River of Life, metal plates and magnetic vapors, letters of healing, pyramid wire contraptions, and the printed hand of alleged divine healers.

The list of trash products used by preachers goes on and on. Some bring in big money. One such piece was a "Holy Shower Cap." This cap was a cheap plastic piece worn by the gullible, then wrapped around some cash or a check and mailed back to the evangelist. This gimmick brought in $100,000 from a single mailing.

Also, "Holy Gloves" (throw-away vinyl work gloves), golden poverty envelopes, special red faith strings, gold and silver lame patches, holy ribbons, blessed shoe liners, sanctified handprints, Russian rubles, red felt hearts, and sacred handkerchiefs embedded with the preacher's sweat.

Former Peter Popoff's assistant Mike Delaney remembers that he delivered several $120,000 checks to a professional letter writer who is still active in that trade. He writes the same valuable junk, inventing crisis situations for big named evangelists.

All of these gimmicks are done in the name of Jesus to assure confidence for financial and physical blessings. There is no divine healing power in these gimmicks. The money sent to T.V. evangelists for these gimmicks plants the seed money into the ministry of that T.V. evangelist. It seems they never suggest any other field to plant the seed.

It is a mystical practice when the evangelist, with extended hand to the camera, decrees to the millions, "Be healed in the name of God."

The evangelist knows that everybody will not be healed; if so, all of America would be in good health by now. The success rate of the psychological results from this mystic style of suggestion probably has the same low percentage as any other type of suggestions.

Another form of suggestion is MENTALISM which teaches that, "God is the mental or intellectual principle that rules all things. Mental Science assumes that mind and not matter is an actual reality and that the illusion of matter can be controlled by mental powers."

Mentalism is nothing more than a sophisticated version of the "power of positive thinking." The "confession doctrine" is propagated by the FAITH movement, known as "Name it and claim it."

Mental healing is accomplished by suggestion or auto suggestion therapy. "Suggestion" is effective whether it is by a shaman, psychic, divine healer or mentalist, or even a situation.

Because of his optimistic attitude about himself and his activities, the believer in MENTALISM gets positive results. The person most likely to succeed in life and in business are those who believe. This type of believing includes the many positive mental attitude groups and such. Mentalism is almost identical to the "confession movement" and Christian Science.

The affirmation, the denial, the platitude, and the decree characterize the confession movement's doctrine, as the following anecdote illustrates:

A prominent citizen of an Oregon town was an ardent believer in the cult of mental healing. Wherever possible this gentleman, with the zeal of a devotee, preached his doctrine. One day on the main street he hailed an impressionable youth from the country. "Billy, " he said, "how's your daddy?"

"Oh," said the youth, "paw's mighty bad off. He's been feelin' poorly all spring. Now he's down flat in bed and ailin' stiddy. We're feared paw's powerful sick. He's feared, too."

"Nonsense," snorted the old man. "Your father isn't sick. He only thinks he's sick. Tell him I said so."

"Yes sir, I will."

A fortnight later the same pair met again in the same place. "Billy," said the citizen cheerfully, "how's your father now?"

Heaving a deep sigh, the youngster replied, "He thinks he's dead."

The sequel to this mentalism by adherents of the confession movement is similar. They insinuate that "everybody should experience health, wealth, and happiness." The confession movement will decree blessings irrespective of God's will. An example of this is, "In the name of Jesus, I command you now to be healed. I decree it!"

These mystical practices have found a place in charismatic religion. Little did some of us in the past suspect that we were parroting the Christian Science doctrine. Someone said in truth, "Christian Science is neither Christian nor Science."

The problem with these four practices of mentalism is that it ignores the sovereignty of God. Briefly, a statement from our mind and lips does not establish truth or put God on hold or in bondage.

Hypnotic therapy also belongs to the class of mental healing. Hypnosis is a *mechanical art*, not a spiritual mystery as many believe.

Hypnosis is the technique of creating an artificial receptivity in the mind. A hypnotic suggestion can assimilate the intellect and correct character defects.

People can be hypnotized by a charismatic personality who presents an artificial package for healing, success, and such. The gullible may believe this artificial suggestion. Mystic mentalism is a mind trip only, and it is artificial. The gullible can accept a mental experience as a spiritual experience.

This "mind trip" looks, sounds, and appears good. Mentalism appears godly, to some, but the missing ingredient for spirituality is commitment to Jesus Christ. The trustful believe every suggestion from falling out, to becoming rich, to spontaneous miracles.

People do believe the suggestions from others (anybody who can get them to believe) to receive immediately all kinds of miracles. But the balanced Christian receives the Word, Wisdom, and Will of God from the pages of the written Word of God. This Word is applied by the Spirit, and that is not a "suggestion"; it is the real living Word of God.

The PSYCHOSOMATIC or faith experience can cure certain ailments. It can be activated by a device, relic, person, or even a situation.

What methods the "quack" uses are irrelevant to a degree. Mega-doses of vitamins, irradiation with colored lights, sugar pills, pushing one over by pressing on the forehead, wearing a copper bracelet, being anointed with water, or chanting magical phrases...all will appear to be effective in the progress of the disease.

When the patient goes through the see-saw experience that occurs in every illness, the healer seems effective and the victim is often deceived. In every case the "quack" cannot be proved wrong and gets the credit in many instances.

It often happens that when one starts going to church, the previous pattern of thinking is arrested. New paths are developed; the old life is not supported; and a new thought pattern is developed. Among other blessings, good health can result. In fact, good health is often accomplished even though this person has never accepted Christ as his Savior. Consider the following story:

A medical doctor says to his patient, "My

friend, what you need is a new place to live."

The doctor is very likely terminating the case for lack of knowledge to help the man further. There is nothing else he could do for his patient.

He moves to Colorado and gets out of the rut that caused his sickness and disease. He loves the place, the fresh air, the new faces, and the friends. He received this new wonderful change with joy.

One day, a hale and hearty fellow hollers and waves to his old doctor. "Don't you know me? I'm the one you gave up on ten years ago."

What happened? Changes brought the shifting of the personality. He developed new mental and emotional patterns. The same happened to the fellow who just joined the church. He noticed after a while that his inflammatory rheumatism cleared up. His new religious zeal and some mending of his ways resulted in his healing. It happens all the time.

There are two essential requirements for the healer to be effective with the sick: The healer has to administer treatment, and the treatment must be harmless.

The quack healer has the advantage, even if the sickness is terminal, acute, or chronic - and especially when the patient recovers.

We are assuming that the "healer's" efforts have no effect on the condition of the patient. There are four courses all sicknesses follow: the patient may die immediately; the patient may linger a long time and then die; the patient may linger a long time, then get well; and the patient may get well immediately.

If the patient dies immediately, the quack says, "Well he just did not start believing soon enough," or "His faith level was not high enough."

If the patient lingers for a long time, then recovers, the quack says, "The prayer of faith was applied. We believed God. Hallelujah! He has never failed us."

When the patient gets well immediately, then he claims, "We got our miracle!"

In every case, the quack is never proved wrong. Any method used will seem to be of value, especially since it is not harmful in any way. The faith healer cannot lose.

Professor Buckland the distinguished biologist of the early 19th Century, gave a dinner one day after dissecting a Mississippi alligator. "How do you like the soup?" asked the doctor after having finished his own plate, addressing a famous gourmand of the day.

"Very good, indeed," answered the other. "Turtle, is it not? I only ask because I do not find any green fat."

The doctor shook his head.

"I think it has somewhat of a musky taste," said another, "not unpleasant but peculiar."

"All alligators have," replied Dr. Buckland. "The fellow I dissected this morning, and whom you have just been eating..."

There was the general rout of guests. Everyone turned pale. Half a dozen started up from the table and hurriedly left the room.

"See what imagination is!" exclaimed Dr. Buckland. "If I had told them it was turtle or terrapin, or bird's nest soup, they would have pronounced it excellent."

"Tell me, doctor, was it really an alligator?"

"Alligator!" laughed the doctor. "Stuff and nonsense...it was nothing but good calf meat."

7

THE WHITE MAGICIAN

John Camp was the spokesman on the special T.V. program, *The Evangelist* aired on April 13, 1988. Viewers were asked to phone in their opinion of Jimmy Swaggart's return to the pulpit. The statement made by John Camp at the end of the program was "The tragedy, in this story of a fall from grace, is not limited to its main character, Jimmy Swaggart. More tragic is the shattered faith of many of his followers in a ministry dominated by the spell-binding power of a single personality. Large numbers have put their faith in this man, not the message."

The words "faith in this man, not the message" point to where the real problem is and always has been...faith in man and not the Gospel of the Lord Jesus Christ!

A Scripture to ponder these days is Matthew 7:22, 23: "Many will say to me in that day, Lord, Lord, have we not prophesied in thy name? and in thy name have cast out devils? and in thy name done many wonderful works? And then will I profess unto them, I never knew you: depart from me, ye that work iniquity." (KJV)

The Greek word for "KNEW" here is "GENOSKO." The word suggests "I have never known you in an "APPROVING" connection." Adam Clarke's commentary says, "You held the truth in unrighteousness, while you preached my pure and holy doctrine; and for the sake of my own truth, and through My love to the souls of men, I blessed your preaching. But yourself I could never esteem, because you were destitute of the spirit of My gospel, unholy in your hearts, and unrighteous in your conduct. Depart from me! - Adam Clarke

In Matthew 25:11, 12 the word "KNOW" is used again, but with a different connotation: "Afterward came also the other virgins, saying, Lord, Lord, open to us. But he answered and said, Verily I say unto you, I know you not." (KJV)

The Greek word for "KNOW" here in Matthew 25 is "OIDA," or "you stand in "NO RELATION" to me."

A Bible illustration of a close relationship is recorded in Matthew 7. Referring to Joseph and Mary, in Matthew 1:25 the scripture says, "And he knew her not..."

The "KNEW" here is "GENOSKO, " as in Matthew 7:23. Joseph was associated with Mary but not intimate with her. They had never known each other in a close marital (sexual) relationship.

In the future judgment, the people that prophesied, cast out devils, and had done many wonderful works, did not have a close relationship with Jesus. They were acquainted with Jesus; He was acquainted with them. But they were not "close." He *never* knew them!

They did not give Jesus first place; they took the glory and credit for themselves. The result? "I never knew you [closely]: depart from me, ye that work iniquity."

White magicians use the names of the Trinity, Bible phrases, and religious symbols. They are guilty of the divination of theomancy. In II Corinthians 11:3-5 Paul says , "But I am afraid that just as Eve was deceived by the serpent's cunning, your minds may somehow be led astray from your sincere and pure devotion to Christ. For if someone comes to you and preaches a Jesus other than the Jesus we preached, or if you receive a different spirit from the one you received, or a different gospel from the one you accepted, you put up with it easily enough. But I do not think I am in the least inferior to those 'super-apostles.' '' (NIV)

Kurt Kotch says the psychological results of BLACK and WHITE magic are the same!

Dr. Diepgen says that magic belongs to neither "theology" nor "medicine."

There are three classes of magic according to Professor Diepgen in his book *Meddizin and Kultur*. These are magic with the help of demons; religious magic which borrows its means from the thought field of the religious outlook (white magic); and natural magic, fully natural, although not fully understood.

Romans 16:17, 18 states, "I urge you, brothers, to watch out for those who cause divisions and put obstacles in your way that are contrary to the teaching you have learned. Keep away from them. For such people are not serving our Lord Christ, but their own appetites. By smooth talk and flattery they deceive the minds of naive people." (NIV)

White magic is stimulated by "a spirit of error," which stems from unscriptural practices. It is divining with the Scriptures. All superstitious occult practices are counterfeits of genuine spiritual gifts. A counterfeit is not a replica; it is an imitation likely to be mistaken for something of higher value. But a "replica" is a close reproduction by the maker of the original. God reveals only the real. Man's counterfeit (something likely to be mistaken for something of higher value) is not a replica; it is more likened to a faint, fuzzy, carbon copy. The reason is a word of knowledge comes from the Holy Spirit, and man's word of knowledge is spoken from the mouth and mind of man. Man cannot even produce a faint, fuzzy, carbon copy. The two are not similar because one originates from man and the other, from the Holy Spirit. The discerning Christian can discern the difference when grounded in the Word.

White magic - like all superstition - should be avoided. Two hundred thousand Americans supposedly carry a rabbit's foot.

White magicians do not expect miracles of raising the dead. His feats are to surpass the laws of nature in a relative way. If miracles did happen, it would help propel his career. When cancer goes into remission, cripples walk, blind men see, and the deaf hear, the white magician will take the credit.

The "laying on of hands," a scriptural method, is misdirected by white magicians. Faith is directed to man's personality rather than to Jesus. A white magician might talk in tongues during his preaching. Doing this without an interpretation (I Cor. 14:28) is forbidden in the Scriptures. It brings clout to the flesh (himself and some in the congregation) for the white magician to burst forth in a jabber adding in a well-learned pentecostal shuffle of the feet. This, done in the general pentecostal convention type circles, spotlights the man rather than the Gospel message. People place ministers in the spotlight like "cult leaders."

The white magician depends on COINCIDENCE - like hitting the bull's eye out of many misses. He thrives on the "hits." And COMBINATION: One may intensely grasp a situation and be able to think it through to the end of the process. A clairvoyant gift is a combination at first sight, in which intervening steps of logical thoughts are passed over. This flash thinking, a short-circuit happening, grasps the situation.

Some might ask, "Does God use coincidence and combination in the manifestation of the gifts?" (I Cor. 12:8)

No! Coincidence and combination cannot energize the gifts.
The Holy Spirit imparts a spiritual knowledge which is not a natural event.

The white magician uses the same techniques as the fortune- teller and astrologer: 1. Observation of the sensory clues. 2. Prior knowledge of subjects obtained secretly before the reading. 3. Ability to think on one's feet and change the direction of the reading without hesitation. 4. Understanding of human nature. 5. An element of luck and a keen sense of playing the odds. A well-placed guess may produce spectacular results, as the following story shows:

An astrologer foretold the death of a lady whom Louis XI passionately loved. She did in fact die, and the King imagined that the prediction of the astrologer was the cause of it. He sent for the man, intending to have him thrown through the window as a punishment. "Tell me, thou pretendest to be so clever and a learned man, what fate will be?"

The soothsayer, who suspected the intrigues of the King and knew his foibles, replied, "Sire, I foresee that I shall die three days before your majesty."

The King believed him and was careful with the astrologer's life.

The psychological principles used by fortune-tellers can fool some people to think the are reading their mind, and white magicians using psychological principles can make people believe they are hearing "a word of knowledge!"

Divine healers (an unfortunate term) who are unsound in their teachings concerning the gifts should be avoided. Their erratic practices are tinged with the occult and superstition. Persons claiming to be divine healers, are deceitful and full of the spirit of error. The Bible does not teach that man heals.

The "NAME OF JESUS" is not a password or magic formula. Jesus must be stamped on our character and engraved on our heart. If not, the name "JESUS" is spoken in vain. One is of "the spirit of error" when JESUS' name is used for selfish gains.

Samuel Hugh Moffett gives an analogy of the way "man" thinks:

When Lawrence of Arabia came to the PARIS PEACE CONFERENCE he brought with him Arab chieftains who had never seen running water. They came from a land where water was scarce and greatly valued.

In the hotel room was a seemingly endless supply of this precious water. By merely turning the tap, they had a vast supply of water, they thought. When they were preparing to leave Paris, Lawrence found them trying to detach the faucet so that out in the dry desert, they would always have water.

Lawrence tried to explain to them that water was not in the faucet, but in huge reservoirs many miles away. They were convinced, however, that there was something magical about the faucets themselves.

So it is with many ministries that direct attention to the leader or founder. These empires are built for the memory of man. But Jesus is the reservoir, and we are the faucets that will soon be off the scene. Only Jesus will remain. "Praise God from whom all blessings flow."

The Holy Spirit cannot be used the way a ventriloquist uses a dummy. The Holy Spirit uses and anoints us "severally as He wills." In John 16:13 we read, "...he will guide you into all truth: for he shall not speak of himself; but whatsoever he shall hear, that shall he speak..." (KJV)

This passage from the original uses the word, "from," rather than the word "of" in this verse. The English translation of the Greek words is, "He shall not speak FROM himself." It is important to understand this scripture.

The limitation usually put on verse 13 is that the Holy Spirit will not speak of Himself, only about Jesus.

The Spirit never exceeds the bounds of God's revealed Written Word in His ministry of teaching and guidance. He shall not speak from Himself, but from the Written Word of God: "...he shall not speak for himself; but whatsoever he shall hear, that shall he speak..."

The practical application of this verse is the Holy Spirit will speak or illuminate only that which He hears from God, Jesus, the Word. Be rest assured, the Holy Spirit will speak nothing more than the authoritative Scripture.

8

TO LIE OR NOT TO LIE: THAT IS THE QUESTION!

In II Timothy 4:2-4 we read, "Preach the Word; be prepared in season and out of season; correct, rebuke and encourage - with great patience and careful instruction. For the time will come when men will not put up with sound doctrine. Instead, to suit their own desires, they will gather around them a great number of teachers to say what their itching ears want to hear. They will turn their ears away from the truth and turn aside to myths." (NIV)

Once when a group visited Lincoln and urged emancipation before he was ready, he argued that he could not enforce it even if he proclaimed it. He gave them this analogy:

"How many legs will a sheep have if you call a tail a leg?" asked Lincoln.

"Five," they answered.

"You are mistaken," said Lincoln. "For calling a tail a leg don't make it so."

A hoax is an untruth deliberately concocted to masquerade the truth. A hoax can be distinguished from honest errors and judgment to which everyone is subject.

The calling card for the ministry and every Christian must be "truth." Leaders in the Gospel ministry must judge and be judged in light of the Word of God. "Error" must be judged in light of "truth," and that truth is the written Word of God.

The following is an excerpt from an article printed on April 6, 1987: *I Felt Death On Me* by Oral Roberts. This critical editor writes:

> "Oral Roberts's revelations from God are to be compared to those received by Moses in the Old Testament.
>
> "God appeared to Moses in a burning bush when he was a young man, to deliver Israel from bondage. Whether God appeared to Oral at any age, for any reason, is still open.
>
> "Moses did ten unforgettable miracles in Egypt, including turning a river into blood. I saw no miracle in Roberts's healing service in Scottsbluff, Nebraska in 1954 - only a line of sick people twenty yards long when he closed down the service for the night.
>
> "Moses stayed on top of God's Mountain for forty days and nights on two consecutive occasions, eating and drinking nothing, yet came down in fine physical condition with the Ten Commandments. Oral went up into his tower and came down in ten days with laryngitis and $8,000,000.
>
> "I appreciate much of the track record of Oral Roberts. Apparently this was the same feeling of those that came to sit in on the T.V. programs and in the tower. However, I wanted to protest by saying, 'I like what you have done too, Oral, but that is not the question. What I do not think is right, is that you lied about the 'death threat' from God.' "

CNN, *U.S. News, World Report News*, and the Roper Organization polled 1,017 people by phone. Their question concerned religion and the electronic church. Sixty-two percent had unfavorable impressions of those who occupy T.V. screen pulpits. Seventy-five percent said Oral Roberts's death threat was only a clever fund-raising technique. Only twelve percent thought Roberts really believed God told him He would die.

Many letters and phone calls pour in and attest that T.V. viewers find solace, inspiration, and results from the T.V. ministry. However, this does not mean that people are receiving the spiritual answers for their lives.

The majority of T.V. evangelists promote success, power, money, prestige, and beauty. These are not essential to Christian values, yet they appeal to almost everyone.

Many continue to love and give to the television ministries. Others protest that the electronic church is the biggest brain wash going on in America. This is the attitude of the larger percent of Americans. It is a small percent of people in this country who support the electronic church, but it still represents a large number of people.

Twenty-one percent of the households in the country - 32,000,000 viewers in 18,000,000 homes - watch at least six minutes of the top religious programs a week. T.V. preachers wield a mighty clout, yet there is NO REVIVAL. This is not to say that a few lives are not being helped. Just because some people are reporting to be dying of boredom in traditional churches does not eliminate the distortion that is being perpetrated by the electronic church. Jeffrey Hadden said, "It's not taking off by leaps and bounds. Evangelists are competing for the same viewers."

The estimated number is only 13,000,000 rather than the larger numbers reported by some big ministries.

No doubt in the very beginning of Roberts's ministry under the tent, he did not dream he would stoop to using a gimmick.

William Martin, Rice University sociologist, said, "But T.V. success is very seductive. They are people who start off with good motives, but get under pressure to get bigger and to stay on top. They do things that in calmer moments they would not do."

Jim Bakker made the statement that he had created a

monster that ate money.

It is extremely interesting that the same three reasons why people tell a lie are the same reasons people say, "God told me to tell you!"

The three reasons to lie are 1. To increase a sense of importance. 2. To gain an end that otherwise would be denied.

The third reason for the "GOD TOLD ME TO TELL YOU" error is they really can't discern the difference between the truth and a lie.

It is only fair to say that a super spiritual type of person is not necessarily a liar and con artist.

David Lane said, "We have a big problem when someone makes a statement about needing to raise money or his life will end. It's the lowest form of emotional appeal." (Lane is president and general manager of WFAA in Dallas, Texas.)

Christian fund-raisers say the widely publicized plea of Oral Roberts has hurt their efforts to raise money. It has set back their own causes perhaps as much as twenty years.

The matter was much discussed at a conference of fund-raisers from forty states. There were more than six hundred evangelical pastors, ministers, and executives present. The session on *Funding The Christian Challenge* was sponsored by the Christian Stewardship Conference and the Billy Graham Center, both of Wheaton, Illinois.

Wesley Willmer, conference chairman, said Roberts's statement was damaging: "First, it gives people the impression that God is a strong-handed God who directs His people in a strong-handed way. This was evident from the cartoons and columns poking fun at Roberts. This kind of tactic also casts a shadow on the whole industry."

Pollster George Gallup, Jr., whose organization conducted a survey for the conference, said it showed forty percent of Americans think Christian fund-raising approaches are unethical.

Nearly half of the respondents said they thought there had been too many fund raising appeals in the past year.

Jerry Sholes, former employee of Oral Roberts, author of *Give Me That Prime Time Religion* said,

"As difficult as it is to accept...and I had some problems with this myself...the City of Faith is based upon lies. The shocking fact is that Oral Roberts, personally, is responsible for those lies. Further, the nature of the lies...having to do with Oral making statements about how and when God told him to build the City of Faith and even what to name the complex...leaves Oral Roberts open to a rather well deserved public contempt. Because of personal involvement on my part in the promotion of the City of Faith, and because of my participation in various planning and strategy sessions relating to the City of Faith, I know and am witness to the fact that Oral Roberts has personally lied about the City of Faith. Those lies and the nature of them...Oral telling millions of people that God told him to do something...are what made me decide to write this book. Everything in this book, every chapter, would have gone to the grave with me, unrevealed to anyone, if it weren't for this fact."

These are powerful allegations by Jerry Sholes, former Roberts employee.

When preachers and churches fail to stand against a lie that effects the whole world, something is wrong with us!

Preachers, of all people, ought to know baloney when they hear it. We must insist on scriptural practices and stand for "no nonsense in the ministry." If we get to the place where we can't recognize baloney, then the question is, are we dishonest too? We must remember these words: "The truth, and nothing but the truth, so help us God!"

And we must live up to them as the following proverb encourages us to do: "He is not an honest man who has burned his tongue and does not tell the company that the soup is hot." -Anonymous, Yugoslav Proverb

Gimmicks have been used by man, and here again the question is not gimmicks but *TRUTH TELLING*. If the gimmick is used to lie, it is the lie that is wrong, not the gimmick. Any gimmick that promises a spiritual blessing is a lie; for example, "This red string will bring you a blessing."

It is not unusual that healers, fortune-tellers, preachers, and people in the entertainment business often begin to believe in their own powers.

A misunderstood and misused gift is prophecy. Prophecy has erroneously been projected as a special message one gives to someone else - like a personal reading. The fake prophecy ranges from giving someone a call to preach to pronouncing someone healed to using a gimmick to raise money, and so on.

The gift of prophecy is in the Scriptures. I Corinthians 12:10 says, "...to others power to prophesy and preach..." (LB)

W.E. Vine gives this definition of prophecy (Greek, Propheteia): "the speaking forth of the mind and counsel of God."

The greater part of prophecy in the Old Testament was prophetic (Future). However, prophecy is not necessarily foretelling. Prophecy in the New Testament is the fore- telling of the will and mind of God. The complete revelation of God to man is now contained in the Scriptures or the Holy Bible.

The purpose of the Holy Spirit today is the same as always: to edify, comfort, and encourage believers (I Cor. 14:3). This is done mainly when one speaks forth the mind of God under the anointing of the Holy Spirit.

The effect of prophecy upon the unbeliever was to show him the secrets of his own heart. The purpose of forth-telling the mind of God is to convict sin and to constrain to worship. As I Corinthians 14:24 and 25 states, "But if all prophesy, and there come in one that believeth not, or one unlearned, he is convinced of all, he is judged of all: And thus are the secrets of his heart made manifest..." (KJV)

Today, the anointed preaching of the Written Word of God is the gift of prophecy in operation. The anointing makes the Word real, to the speaker and to some that hear the Spirit speak.

This "prophecy" in chapter one by Oral Roberts while in the Prayer Tower, is not a Bible prophecy, rather "THEOMANCY." (Using the Scriptures to divine.)

The following is also a prophecy by a psychic printed in the *News Weekly World* on June 2, 1987. It is about "the Jim Bakkers," formerly of the P.T.L. Ministry. The article was written by Steven Reyes.

"Psychic Countess Sophia Sabak's prophecy included:

1. Jim and Tammy will come back bigger and better than ever.

2. Stardom is the Bakkers destiny, and they couldn't deny it even if they wanted to, said the countess. I've had vision after vision about them ever since their PTL ministry hit the skids.

3. Singing star Tammy will make the cross over from Gospel to Country and Pop.

4. Jim will enter politics. He has the charisma, energy, and intelligence to become a top law maker, said the countess.

"Sabak says, With the money from supporters rolling in, I see the Bakkers bankrolling a Christian retreat like PTL's Heritage, U.S.A. only bigger and better. I think they'll probably call it 'Hallelujah City' in honor of their comeback and the man upstairs, who made their stunning new success possible."

These words of Oral Roberts in the tower and psychic Sabak are nothing but man's word, featured as a supernatural word event.

It seems that God changes His mind often with those who are always getting a "God told me to tell you." Oral Roberts was a guest on the Larry King Show on August 23, 1987 on CNN. Roberts apologized to Jimmy Swaggart and the Assemblies of God because of some unfounded statements he had made in his "the Lord is in my mouth" prophecy. The reason for this apology on nationwide T.V. was more information had come out about the guilt of the Bakkers. He apologized explaining the reason for his mistake: "Because I did not know what they knew."

Looking back, Oral would not have apologized to Swaggart, if he had known what Jimmy Swaggart knew even then and what we all know now.

If God had told Roberts then God would need to be the one apologizing, for a direct quote from Oral is "the Word of the Lord is in my mouth."

"This very prominent ministry and the headquarters of a very prominent denomination (Jimmy Swaggart and The Assemblies of God) have formed an unholy alliance," Roberts said.

It can't be spoken any plainer than that! If the prophecy had come from the Lord, it would not have had to be taken back.

9

SORCERY - - - WHAT IS IT?

"So My hand will be against the prophets who see false visions and utter lying divinations. They will have no place in the council of My people, nor will they be written down in the register of the house of Israel, that you may known that I am the Lord God. It is definitely because they have misled My people by saying, 'Peace!' when there is no peace. And when anyone builds a wall, behold, they plaster it over with white-wash; so tell those who plaster it over with whitewash, that it will fall..." (Ezekiel 13:9-11) (NAS)

Sorcery is a superstitious tool of Satan pretending employment of supernatural agencies. Here is a list of most superstitions and occult practices: amulets, astrology, black and white magic, charming, Christian Science, clairvoyance, color therapy, death magic, eye diagnoses, fanaticism, fetishes, fortune-telling, ghosts, heresies, hypnosis, letters of protection, magical healing methods, mental suggestion, mesmerism, modern theology, numerical symbolism, occult literature, omens, palmistry, psycho analysis, psychography, psychometry, significant dates and days, spiritualism, superstition, telepathy, transference, wart removal, witch-craft, psychomachy, theomancy, hex signs, and channeling.

Superstitions are widespread, and certain signs bring on certain beliefs. Here are some examples: an itchy nose means company is coming; a cat's eating grass is a sign of rain; walking under a ladder is bad luck; the ace and queen of spades signify death; a knife sticking in the floor means disaster; a ringing in the ears means either bad news or someone is talking about someone; the barn owl's cry means death; the cuckoo's call means a wish is fulfilled; the green woodpecker's cry is a sign of rain; a raven on the roof heralds bad luck; and seeing a magpie implies sorrow.

Upon no subject has it been so easy to deceive as through the title of this chapter. Every person has a curiosity to a greater or lesser degree. People want to know all about one's self and the future. This curiosity of man is what keeps the sorcerers in business.

Another gimmick of sorcery is the stunt called "STICHOMANCY." This form of divination is letting the Bible fall open in order to receive divine direction. It is well established in religion. The Greeks did it with Homer. The Moslems did it with the *Koran*.

The following are three species of divination given by Gaule in his Magastromancer. The total list is quoted in *Hone's Year Book*, page 1517.

"Divination by: PSYCHOMANCY is divination by soul, affections, or dispositions of man; ONEIROMANCY is to divine by dreams; THEOMANCY is to divine through the delusion, by the revelation of the Spirit, and by the Scriptures. (The Word of God.)"

"...we have renounced secret and shameful ways; we do not use deception, nor do we distort the word of God...For we do not preach ourselves, but Jesus Christ as Lord..." (II Cor. 4:2, 5) (NIV)

All forms of divination over the past five thousand years bear testimony of man's tainted belief. It is a universal diffusion that one can read another person with skill.

The belief that one can read another person by "a word of knowledge" (I Cor. 12:8) is fallacy. It is as untrue as Indian dances producing rain.

The white magician may tell his audience that he "feels" the healing power in his hands or use the worn-out phrase "God is speaking to me." This activity and claim is magnetism by one with a "cultic" syndrome. His tactics are as deceptive as the new paint on a second hand car.

In some cases magnetizers use "things" for someone to believe in - minerals, magnets, stones, or crystals that contain magnetic properties. Some white magicians practice animal magnetism when they tell the people they have "power" in their hands.

There was a Mr. Valentine Gretrak, who practiced magnetism. He practiced a deception akin to animal (the person) magnetism, like thepresent-day charisma in religion. He was the son of an Irish gentleman, of good education and property. He fell at an early age into some sort of melancholy derangement. The strange feeling came to him that God had given him the power to cure the King's evil.

He extended his powers to the curing of epilepsy, ulcers, aches, and lameness. He was effective in cases where the disease was heightened by hypochondria and depression of spirits. He set aside three days a week, during which he laid hands upon all who came. The crowds thronged him.

People came from neighboring towns, from all parts of Ireland, and from England. Several of these poor credulous people no sooner saw him than they fell into fits. He restored them by waving his hand in their faces and praying over them. He affirmed that the TOUCH OF HIS GLOVE had driven pains away.

Gretrak imagined that he received his power direct from heaven to throw people into fits. What Gretrak practiced was almost exactly like the fashion of modern day magnetizers.

Early in the 18th century the attention of Europe was directed to a very remarkable instance of fanaticism. This has been claimed by animal magnetists as a proof of their sciences.

A group of people gathered in great numbers round the tomb of their favorite saint. They taught one another how to fall in convulsions. These convulsionaries in St. Medard believed that St. Paris would cure all their infirmities. Hysterical women and weak-minded persons of all descriptions flocked to the tomb from far and near. Working themselves up to a pitch of excitement, they went off one after the other into fits.

The error of Mesmer's delusion is he maintained that the magnetic matter or fluid pervaded all the universe. He taught that every human contained it and could communicate it to another by an exertion of the will. The Academy of Science at Berlin was anything but favorable to his system.

Mesmer amused himself by casting out devils and healing the sick by merely laying hands on them. As Mesmer would lay on his hands, delicate girls fell into convulsions. Hypochondriacs fancied themselves cured. His house was daily besieged by the lame, the blind, and the hysterical. Mesmer also tried his hand upon some paupers in the hospitals of Berne and Zurish. He succeeded, according to his own account. He was not successful in curing an ophthaslmia and a gutta serena.

The present day fake Word of Knowledge is projected as a supposed "remote viewing." "During the crisis, mesmerists are said to posses an extraordinary and supernatural power. When touching a patient presented to them, they can supposedly feel what part of his body is diseased, even by merely passing their hand over the clothes."

Another singularity was that these mesmerist healers could discover diseases by seeing into the interior of other men's stomachs.

According to M. Deleuze, any person could become a magnetizer by conforming to the following conditions and acting upon the following rules:

1. Forget for a while all your knowledge of physics and metaphysics.

2. Remove from your mind all objections that may occur.

3. Imagine that it is in your power to take the malady in hand and throw it on one side.

4. Never reason for six weeks after you have commenced to study.

---

5. Have an active desire to do good, a firm belief in the power of magnetism, and an entire confidence in employing it.

In short, repel all doubts, desire success, and act with simplicity.

That is to say, "be very creditable; be very preserving; reject all past experience; and do not listen to reason." And you are a magnetizer after M. Deleuze's own heart.

The practices of the magnetizer can be compared to the modus operandi of some Charismatics. If one learns healing as an "art," or if one is born with occult powers, it most assuredly is not a "GIFT" of the Holy Spirit.

The following is a portion of a television program aired on May 29, 1978.

NORVELLE HAYS, (Guest): About eighteen years ago I was in Pennsylvania on a cold December night speaking at a fancy banquet in a ballroom, giving my life story when a Pentecostal feller challenged me, from the back. He said, "I've been deaf for thirty years, and God spoke to me and told me to come up here and have you lay your hands on me and pray for me and make this thing leave me." I said, "Well, this is a Christmas banquet, but I'll do it." So I reached down and laid my hands on him, and I said, "You, foul spirit, have stopped his hearing for thirty years; you come out of him." And he fell on the floor the first time I said that, and his ears popped open, and he began to laugh ...I said, "What are you laughing so hard about?" He said, "I never heard a watch tick before!" And all of a sudden (This is the night that changed my whole life), about fifty people at the banquet ran up to me and said "Pray for me," "Pray for me." And I reached out like this to pray for them, and when I did, the whole bunch went s w i s h and fell to the floor. And I said, "Oh my God!" It scared me. I reached out. They were trying to get to me through the seats, and they were praying, and all of them falling. And an old grey- haired pentecostal man eighty-five years old walked up to me and said, "Young man, I haven't seen any power like this in fifty-five years." He said, "I'm an old pentecostal missionary. Fifty-five years ago I saw this in pentecostal circles. I haven't seen anything like this - all these people look like they're all dead. Looks like you shot the whole banquet with a machine gun." I said, "I've never seen it before in my whole life." I've never seen anything like that. But that night, God put His healing power in my hands, and it's been in there ever since.

T.V. HOST: Norvelle Hays, will you pray?

NORVELLE HAYS: Father, in Jesus' name, I reach my hand out, Lord, to this camera. I reach out to America, and I pray the Spirit of God that raised Jesus from the dead, the Spirit of God that came in my hands, Lord, go through that television screen right now, Father, in Jesus' name...I cure all afflictions in Jesus' name. It's [the affliction] not of God; it's of the devil...You can mold them into men and women You want them to be, in Jesus' name, just like You have me and Richard, Oral, Billy, Joe, Cheryl, and Lindsey. You will mold them to be productive.

T.V. HOST (speaking to someone in the T.V. audience): You have not been able to move your hand. You've not been able to open and close your hand. And the pain in your wrist...God is healing you right now. While Norvelle was praying, God began to give me a word of knowledge.

The statements from the the T.V. program include: this is the hand I saw; God put His healing power in my hands; Spirit of God...go through that television screen; I curse all affliction in Jesus' name; and God gave me a word of knowledge.

Many may not think such statements are dangerous, but they are.

Fortune-telling is as fruitless as destiny foretold by the stars.

Simon Magnus practiced SORCERY. He PRETENDED the employment of the supernatural. During the time of Justin Martyr, Simon was regarded as the founder of Christian heresy. Justin himself came from Samaria and knew that Simon was a native of the village of Gitthae. Justin, the Christian theologian had been told that Simon practiced the art of magic at Rome. The senate and the people at Rome had erected a statue in his honor with the inscription "SIMONI DEO SANCTO (To Simon the holy God)."

Simon was credited with numerous feats. According to one legend, he attempted to fly over Rome. Others claimed that he tried to emulate the burial and resurrection of Jesus but did not survive the experience.

Simon's magic was said to produce everything one could desire: invisibility, invulnerability, the animation of statues, tunneling under mountains, and transformation into a sheep or goat. Like Jesus, he was said to have been born of a virgin mother.

Much of this history and legend complies with the scripture in Acts 8:9. It says that he "...bewitched the people of Samaria." *The Living Bible* says, "...in fact, the Samaritan people often spoke of him as the Messiah." (Acts 8:11)

Simon Magnus was still deceived after he was baptized in water (verse 13). He offered money for the power which he saw through the life of Phillip. The Scriptures state in verse 13, "...he continued with Philip, and wondered, beholding the miracles and signs which were done."

After he had been baptized and said, "Give me also this power" (verse 19), Peter said to him, "Repent therefore of this thy wickedness." (verse 22)

Simon was wicked because he had to live in the eyes of men. He had to be in their mouths; he had to have a crowd around him. II Timothy 3:13 describes many in Bible days as well as many today: "But evil men and seducers shall wax worse and worse, deceiving, and being deceived." (KJV)

In Acts 8:20, Peter rebuked Simon Magnus because he thought the gift of God could be purchased with money. In verse 21, Peter tells him, "Thou hast neither part nor lot in this matter: for thy heart is not right in the sight of God." (KJV)

Simon wanted the POWER without JESUS. What was Simon Magnus's sin? He pretended employment of supernatural agencies. What Simon claimed he was doing was not true; he was lying.

Simon was in "error," but there is no indication that he was demon possessed. The clairvoyant girl at Phillippi was not a sorceress; she was, in fact, demon-possessed. She said, "...These men are the servants of the most high God, which shew unto us the way of salvation." (Acts 16:17) (KJV)

What the possessed girl said was true. Paul and others were, in fact, the servants of the most high God. Paul was not disturbed about what she said but where she received her information. She possessed the spirit that "unveiled hidden things in the past, present, and future." She received this information from a spirit not of God, for Paul said, "...I command thee in the name of Jesus Christ to come out of her..." (Acts 16:18) (KJV)

She was possessed by a supernatural spirit from Satan. Paul spoke to the spirit and not to the girl: "... a spirit of divination met us, which brought her masters much gain by soothsaying." (Acts 16:16) (KJV)

The degree of divination practiced by this girl is witchcraft or black magic. It is not mental suggestion, palmistry, or Simon Magnus type of sorcery.

Paul cast the evil spirit out of the girl in Acts 16:18, and he called Simon wicked in Acts 8:22, for his heart was not right with God.

There are many unusual and mysterious happenings that cannot be explained. The "unusual" does not constitute a "real" God-sanctioned experience.

A devout woman whose body was twisted and tortured for twenty years with excruciating pains is now completely healed - thanks to a T.V. blessing from Pope John Paul II. She was bent over, and her joints were swollen twice their normal size. She developed rheumatoid arthritis at the age of thirty. Marya Walicki is now over fifty years old. Marya, of

Wadowice, Poland, says nothing seemed to help her chronic condition.

On bad days she was confined to bed, her joints rigid in pain. "For my birthday, my husband bought me a T.V. How he afforded it, I'll never know. But he said maybe it would take my mind off my pain when I was in bed. I cried. It was so wonderful."

She got up and walked after watching the pope on her television. The headlines of the article read, "Prayers to image of pope on T.V. cure woman of arthritis. Marya's doctor has no explanation for the reversal of her condition, but admits, 'I have never seen so complete a recovery.'" UNUSUAL?

A faith healing cat, cures crippling ailments by the laying on of its paws. The medical and psychic worlds are taken by storm. Dozens of former disease victims attest to the feline's miraculous powers.

Word spread of the amazing kitty's incredible healing feats. Pilgrims from every corner of the globe are flocking to Blackburn, England. They seek relief from everything from hiccups to heart disease. "I can vouch for the cat's awesome abilities," says forty-five year old former ulcer sufferer, Fredrick Van Note of Birgdorf, West Germany. He journeyed to Blackburn after a host of doctors in his own country could not help him.

"I had suffered from bleeding ulcers for five years, and was wracked daily with excruciating pain," he adds, "but when the cat put his paws on my stomach, my gut-splitting torment vanished."

"It isn't magic," Leora (the cat's owner) adds, eyes twinkling. "It's the power of God acting through my cat. Cats are very spiritual beings, you know. Edison (her cat) is very special. God has given him the power to heal!" UNUSUAL?

Dozens of motorists have been frightened and infuriated by a hitchhiking ghost. He scolds them about their driving habits and then vanishes into thin air!

Over forty motorists testify, "One minute he was sitting beside me in the seat, and the next minute he was gone."

Josef Marcak, a factory supervisor from Brno, (Czechoslovakia) said, "There was no way he could have got out of the car. I was driving sixty miles per hour."

Over the years hitchhiking ghosts have been encountered in virtually every civilized country in the world. The Czechoslovakian ghost is believed to be the first, however, to scold motorists for their driving. UNUSUAL?

Professional exorcists say fighting the devil is all in a day's work. Harry Kuboi uses a blaring trumpet, salt water, and a wooden cross in his daily battle with the devil. He is a paid professional exorcist.

With his horn and his own brand of "holy" water, Harry wrestles Satan out of humans for $100. He saves homes from the prince of darkness, too.

A mysterious child-healer cures disease by absorbing symptoms directly from his patients into his own body - and then returning to normal in a matter of minutes.

Witnesses say, "He places his hands on his patient, closes his eyes, and mutters a prayer.

"I have seen his hands thicken and blacken as he treated a poor leper. Last year while healing a paralyzed woman, he lost all feeling and movement in his body. After some minutes of this, he gives a shudder and returns to perfect health. It's clearly real, not a pretense."

The child is believed to be endowed by Buddha with power to banish disease. Priests and mystics have taken up residence near his home. UNUSUAL?

"And now, if you take possession of the golden cross at once - see how quickly your own miracles come true! Read how it brought thousands of dollars, a new house, a sensational job, and much more to people just like you." (Magazine article)

Think about this miraculous "power" of the hallowed earth of Fatima. The Roman Catholic world still trembles from the vision seen by three shepherd children.

A church painting sobs real tears! Thousands of eyewitnesses look on in amazement! In the first week more than 10,000 people filed into the church to stare at the weeping Madonna's glistening tears.

110

Father Koufos says, "Several streams of moisture were flowing downward from the eyes of the Virgin. As we backed off stunned, streams spewed from both hands. Puddles of tears began to collect on the floor. We fell to our knees, overwhelmed. Some of the women helping with the preparations began to sob and pray."

Father Koufos put wads of cotton under the icon to absorb the liquid. Later he lit an incense burner. UNUSUAL?

Nostradamus was the crown prince of prophecy, known as the greatest predictor of all time. He was raised a Christian. He was nicknamed "the little astrologer." As a physician he healed the sick and concocted health potions. His brilliant and accurate predictions were so obliquely worded they could mean virtually anything.

He predicted marvels of science, including a manned space station circling 270 miles above the earth. He made it clear that his predictions extend to the year 3797. UNUSUAL?

In Shanghai China, there is a pond of water that thousands think is MAGIC! The newspaper says, "Up to 10,000 people a day continue to flock to the pond to sip the water. Thousands report its miraculous cures." UNUSUAL?

The following is a modern day example of sorcery or the pretending of the supernatural. This type of sorcery is kin to theomancy or "divination pretending to divine by the revelation of the spirit and by the Scriptures or the Word of God."

As did millions, we received a plastic container (with a financial appeal) that contained water. On the little bag, about one-and-a-half inches square, was printed "River of Life Anointed Water. Do not drink this."

The computer letter printed to appear personal included the following information.

"Are you ready to be cleansed through God's miracle working power? God has sent me as His prophet to tell you how to get the answers to your needs. His perfect plan began back in 1977 when he gave me a vision.

"He (God) told me to build a 777-foot River of Life representing the River of Life in heaven that is talked about in Revelations 22:1 and 2. Now, God has jolted my spirit and made me to know He had me build that symbol of the River of Life not just for looks, BUT FOR YOUR HEALING.

This healing stream is joined to the city by the sixty-foot bronze sculpture. God has called us to have a miracle-healing service on June 22 for your healing, in the River of Life. My son and I have prayed over the River of Life enough to believe GOD'S HEALING ANOINTING IS NOW IN THOSE WATERS. I have instructed our associates to put some of THE ANOINTED WATER INTO THE SMALL CLEAR BAG I HAVE SENT TO YOU who cannot be at the healing service on June 22.''

The letter instructs as follows: "Write 7 things that you want us to pray for on June 22. On June 22, I want you to open your bag of anointing water from the River of Life and anoint something that is symbolic of your need. Anoint your billfold if you have a financial need. Anoint your body if you have a physical need.''

Note: A form was included in the promotion, so the victim could write down his requests. Printed in bold type on the paper was, "Pastor, I'm believing for my miracle as I plant my seed of $7.00, $17.00, or other $_____.''

This appeal in beautiful, four-color printing was sent with a financial appeal. "God's healing anointing is now in those waters,'' was the direct quote of the evangelist.

Ministers of the Gospel stoop to such tactics to reap financial gain only. Josh Billings said, "Ambition is like hunger; it obeys no law but its appetite.''

Why do large numbers of people fall for this "THEOMANCY"? The simple answer is "The head, like the stomach, is easily infected with poison when it is empty.''
-Richter

All fortune-telling is condemned in the Written Word of God. Whether astrology, crystal ball gazing, fortune cookies, a religious giving a personal reading (using Scriptures), or a reader using tea leaves, the results are the same. Any and all types of readings will bring about the same results as Kickapoo Indian medicine.

10

WHAT HAS HAPPENED
TO US?
IS THERE A REAL?

The growing group of charismatic pentecostals is an irrepressible army for evangelism. Regarding their vision and progress, the charismatic crowd endeavors to follow the New Testament pattern for reaching the world.

Perhaps it has been twenty years since the great outpouring of the Holy Spirit among the mainline denominational churches. For example, there was a spiritual awakening among the Catholics at Dequine University. Priests, nuns, and laity made personal confessions to Jesus Christ for the repentance of sins. They asked Him literally to become their personal Savior. It was the beginning of the Charismatic Renewal in the Catholic Church. Many began to read the Bible and followed the Lord in believer's baptism.

Many wonderful things have happened in the old line churches. There have been conversions, baptisms of the Holy Spirit, witnessing, and so on. It is no wonder that Satan and his demons are invading this movement trying to nullify all the good things that came out of this tremendous revival. Like the children of Israel, they didn't know how to control or handle their new-found freedom in Christ. Now this movement is in turmoil and has been set back many times because of UNCONTROLLED pentecostalism. Free worship, it seems for some, has led to free-thinking concerning Bible interpretation. This spirit gives birth to unscriptural, unregulated activities that spring out of man, ignoring Biblical directions.

Our staggering gains through converting, baptizing, and spreading the faith are sometimes hindered because of our disregarding the sovereignty of God. This is a battle that we must constantly be aware of and fight. I too have had opportunities to embrace this doctrine and many times have been tempted, but, by the grace of God, I haven't. We have often been guilty of placing subjective experiences above "Thus saith the Lord." As a result, many in the ministry of reconciliation have lost esteem and spiritual credibility.

Two of the "beliefs" that have brought discredit to the charismatics are these: THE CONFESSION DOCTRINE, which is a simplified version of Christian Science; it is the attitude that regardless of the will, wisdom, or Word of God, men can decree God to perform, to man's desires. GIFT THEOLOGY, primarily "a word of knowledge" misunderstood and mishandled, has been tagged "Charismatic Fortune-Telling." The self-appointed prophet can declare almost anything under the guise that God told him. This style of prophecy is a heyday for those who operate with an open-end policy to parrot God to say almost anything one chooses.

At Calvary Assembly of God I have tried to work in the contents of ethics and scriptural delivery of the truth. The freewheeling evangelist wants to sell himself; the "real man of God" recommends the whole council of God using the Bible as his only authority.

I received a request from one of my church members who was seriously ill to visit him at his home. He is a retired staff sergeant of the U.S. Army. As I drove down the interstate to a little suburb, I was praying that I might be of some help. He had been under the surgeon's knife five times in the past two-and-a-half years.

As I approached the door, I prayed, asking God to guide my every word. I knew this man did not have long to live. I rang the door bell. When the door opened, there stood the man, slightly bent over because of a recent major surgery. He directed me to sit down in the front room.

He told me of the doctor's frightening diagnosis. "Pastor, let me tell you how I feel and what I believe. You tell me if I am right."

I said, "O.K., John."

Through his tears he began. "I accepted the Lord Jesus Christ as my personal Savior when I was a young person. I have never turned against the Lord. Though I have made mistakes, I am considered a good, moral man. I know that I am saved, by grace, and I trust in nothing but the blood of Jesus Christ for salvation. Though I do not feel good about all of my life, I trust Jesus Christ. Other than Him, there is no hope. Pastor, I have just been cut open again. This surgery two weeks ago was my fifth surgery in the military hospital. The doctors took the clamps off only yesterday. They discovered they could not help me and just sewed me back up. Pastor, I'm going to die, and I need to talk with someone for spiritual help."

By now he could no longer control his sobs, and he went into another room to regain his composure. When he came back into the front room, he said, "I'm sorry about this emotion. I have always been strong, able to face life. But now, I am weak and sick."

He weighed twenty to thirty pounds less than the picture on the wall indicated he had at one time weighed.

I began counseling this distraught man seeking spiritual strength and physical healing, but at the same time he asked and I agreed to hold his funeral service. What a dilemma when one is face to face with a man who is dying, praying for healing, and discussing his funeral arrangements all at the same time. This would no doubt be called a "negative confession" by many. The faith healers would say I wasn't exercising - nor was he - any faith what-so-ever!

I knew that without a miracle from God, this man was dead. I know beyond a shadow of a doubt that God still heals today. Every fiber within me cries that out from the pulpit. Hebrews 13:8 says that He gives miracles as always: "Jesus Christ the same yesterday, and today, and for ever."

Those diagnosed "hopeless" need not despair, but need rather to go to God, for He is our source. The fact is, and I was faced with that stark reality in that living room, that I have never healed anyone. I would if I could, but I do not have, nor does any other living man, the gift to heal others. The choice for healings and miracles belongs to our sovereign God. He alone heals "severally as He wills."

It is time that we face the truth and the reality of the Word of God. No one, absolutely no one except Jesus Christ, has ever possessed the power to perform a miracle or to heal.

Let's face the truth: No one except Jesus has ever possessed the power to perform miracles and to heal.

The freewheeling evangelist sells himself, mostly, over television or in front of the thousands in an auditorium. The ordained resident minister pastors mostly in small groups and one-to-one counselling sessions. The "healer" offers a transmission of heavenly power through his hands and speaks his word of knowledge "straight out of heaven." However, an examination of the facts proves faith healers do not bring the quality results reported. The usual result is that people have not been healed of their sickness and leave the meeting with only a lighter pocketbook.

If I had embraced the confession doctrine, I would have told this very sick man to just confess it as done. I knew that was not the scriptural way. I also knew that the philosophy preaches pretty good at times, but when you are looking one in the face knowing full well that it does not work, you cannot use such a gimmick. Faith teaching, by many, is much like a magical charm. It is a faith that attempts to force God to act, regardless of His will.

As our conversation drew to an end about the arrangements he wanted to make for his funeral, I knew that I couldn't leave his house without praying a prayer of faith for his healing. I bowed my head and asked Jesus Christ to touch his body and to bring healing to it. Knowing that there wasn't anything else that I could do, I left. I left him in the hands of

God. That was now over a year ago, and he is still alive. So I do know and I believe without a doubt that I serve a miracle-working God and One who does heal. But I do not heal. I give all of the praise to Jesus Christ, his healer.

In 1956 in Miami, Florida, Evangelist Jack Coe was arrested and stood trial. Doctors accused him of dangerously proclaiming people healed who were not healed. Jack Coe insisted that braces be taken off the legs of a little crippled boy.

But Jack Coe, who taught that it was God's will to heal everybody and that only the lack of faith prevented healing, died of bulbar polio.

I remember as a young pastor listening to the radio every night for the report about Rev. Coe's condition. We do not rejoice because of a person's death, but the point being made is that *many* who preach and teach that all Christians in every situation will be healed if they do not doubt are in error.

Many can be added to the list. Dr. John Roach Stratton of the famous Calvary Baptist Church, New York was a most ardent advocate of complete healing for the body. But Dr. Stratton sickened and died. Dr. A.B. Simpson, a noble man of God, was the founder of the Christian and Missionary Alliance. He also made much of divine healing, but eventually Dr. Simpson himself sickened and, after a long period of depression, died.

Mrs. Aimme Semple McPherson had great crowds all over America and particularly in the Angelus Temple in Los Angeles. She too laid great emphasis on the healing of the body and stressed that it was always God's will to heal the sick. She taught that only unbelief would prevent the healing. And yet she was sick, treated in a hospital, and she eventually died.

Dr. Alexander Dowie made much of healing and without doubt was a good, sincere man. He would take train loads of people to other cities and pray for the sick in his campaigns. I do not remember the source, but I read that he prayed for rain in a parched desert area. And while he prayed, it began to rain! In later years, however, he became fanatical, fell into disrepute, brought reproach upon the cause of Christ, and died a disillusioned man.

117

One of the pastors when I was a boy was Evangelist A.A. Allen. I preached three revivals for Rev. Allen's wife when she was pioneering a church in Texas. He too proclaimed the faith message as these others. However, Rev. Allen, according to the *San Francisco Examiner*, died in front of a television set in his fourth floor suite in San Francisco. The coroner, Dr. Henry Turkel, said that he had died of "acute alcoholism and fatty infiltration of the liver."

Healers slyly project the idea that they personally possess the nine gifts of the Spirit. This teaching is unsound.

The front room situation is different from the big crowd scene. The preacher calls down the Lord hot and heavy proclaiming, "God is showing me through a Word of Knowledge, He is healing someone here of cancer."

As he preached to a live audience and to the millions on T.V. (Trinity Broadcasting Network in California), R. W. Shamback graveled out the words, "God is gonna heal everything here tonight." This popular shot gun method used mostly in large numbers does not work the same with only two in the front room. Since that time the evangelist himself has had open heart surgery.

Statistics bear out that a miracle occurs only on rare occasions. In the lifetime of many ministries a documented miracle is never witnessed.

It is a dishonor to the legitimate ministry when the reports are not "up front." Reporting the supposed successes but never the failures smacks of dishonesty.

In our regular services at Calvary Assembly of God, we almost without exception have our deacons come to the front and obeying the Scripture lay hands on the sick. We have many testimonies of healings that have taken place during these times of prayer.

One particular one was of a lady who had moved to Waco from Dallas, Texas. She came into the church service, feeling the presence of the Lord, and witnessing His Spirit. She had been to the doctor who diagnosed her condition and documented that she had cancer. She had felt the leading of the Lord to come to the front to have the deacons pray for her. One of the deacons of the church laid hands upon her and prayed the prayer of faith. In time she went to the doctor and had an examination. The examination showed that she was completely cured of cancer.

This is just one of the many occasions where God heals and miracles occur. It is a common occurrence in our church and in many other churches. Where the Scripture is obeyed, the sick shall recover.

At the close of a Christian T.V. show videotaping, while shaking hands with members of the studio audience, "the star" stopped to pray for a man. The man looked very sick as if he were moments from death.

The man in the wheelchair was there to see the show before he died. He had not walked in months. After prayer, at "the star's" urging, the man stood up. The people cheered as the man took a couple of very shaky, small steps. While everyone applauded, it seemed the man might fall. The next day the man was shown on national T.V. as a miracle. This type of thing is typical of healers. To report a failure is not typical of the healing con!

This same elderly man was tracked down to see if, in fact, he had been healed, or if the healing had lasted. He had died ten days after his visit to the show.

What is suspicious about this account is that "a miracle" was reported, but the death was not.

Most healers teach "if a miracle is not granted, it is the fault of the supplicant." This heresy (Pelagian) says after one has followed prescribed formulas, if the miracle is not granted, the one asking is at fault. Those who demand favors from God, they say, have every right to do so, and God must grant this boon according to contract.

LET'S HAVE A SPECIAL MEETING!

I invite Oral Roberts, Richard Roberts, Bob Tilton, Kenneth Haggin, Kenneth Copeland, W.V. Grant, Charles Capps, Fred Price, the Hunters, Norvelle Hays, and many more that claim the gift of healing, to come to Calvary Assembly of God Church in Waco, Texas for a special meeting to bless people who are in real desperate physical need.

After all, we should minister to this sector of society who are really helpless. We could, say, assemble one hundred young, believing crippled children into the church; then bus an equal number from the school for the blind; then gather as many deaf mutes into the church. We could also bring those in our nursing centers who are incapable of walking. Here would be a potential crowd of over three hundred people. The efforts could be tripled, and we could easily have a group of a thousand. Our church will hold that many. This group of hopeless and helpless would require genuine, real, physical miracles.

The needs would be visible and already accurately diagnosed by a medical doctor. The bogus "Word of Knowledge" would not have to be used.

The surprisingly large number always standing around healing meetings afflicted with headaches, sore shoulders, poor vision, poor hearing, family problems, and such would not be invited to this meeting. The crowd would include the crippled in the electrically driven chairs, the totally blind, the absolutely deaf, and cripples who can't walk one step. The power of suggestion, the placebo, showmanship, planted people, publicity, success stories, WILL NOT BE THE STANDARD FOR THIS SPECIAL GROUP.

If a daunted, heartsick group like this ever assembles in one place appealing for a miracle, their need could never be questioned. One thing is certain: the healers, shamen, white magicians, and any who claim a gift, I feel, would not appear. Rather than a healer's setting up such a meeting, he would sidestep one.

The only answer for this group would be miracles. Most "healers" would know they could not help, for they have never seen the kind of results needed for these cases. Why? Because no man can heal. The Gifts are resident in the Holy Spirit, not in a human person. He (the Holy Spirit) only can give out miracles and DIVINE HEALING, "severally as HE wills" and not when we COMMAND. If the gifts were resident in the person of man, there would have already been many of these types of gatherings.

Needless to say, the healing evangelist needs the crowd to represent a cross section of all needs to accomplish his desired results. The carnival atmosphere is a requirement for their razzle-dazzle.

The "positive confession" philosophy that all Christians will be healthy, wealthy, and wise preaches good but is not always the factual experience of all genuine Christians.

The "name it and claim it" theory is simply a repeat of the SCIENCE OF MIND ideas of Ernest Holmes. Positive affirmation teaches that by uniting our mind with God's mind (the two become one), we can divinely control our environment and life. Holmes admittedly made up his own religion by combining elements of the occult and Eastern philosophy with the Bible. This teaching is now found among the cults as well as some Christian groups.

Much teaching today claims that faith is something like a magical charm. They teach that we control the divine will of God and force God to act. If you have faith, then God must do as you "believe," regardless of His will.

If positive confession is scripturally correct, why does it fail most of the time? Which healer, evangelist, pastor, teacher, or psychic claims his healing ministry even approaches the quality of Jesus' ministry? True, there are many who are blessed by various ministries. But suggestion or a placebo or self-diagnosis must not be mistaken for a divine healing.

Many Christians are bitter because they were told they were healed when, in fact, they were not. They have "kept the faith," yet remained ill, and some have died! The victim cannot win, and the "healer" always has a "pet" answer for the other person's failure. There is no way to know how much damage has been done, in the name of Christ, even though some ministers have good intentions.

God is a miracle-worker and there is a "real."

Star Daily tells of a boy who was desperately ill with infantile paralysis.

> "The mother arrived at the church, weeping, full of fear. Her minister, Pastor Brown, asked, 'If you knew it was God's will, would you be willing to let Billy go to heaven? Could you give him up if you knew God wanted him?'

"After a long struggle with her emotions, she said, 'Yes, if I knew for certain it was God's will, I'd be willing to release the boy!'

"Pastor Brown then lifted the child up to God in prayer, surrendering him completely to the mercy and wisdom of God. Three days later the boy was discharged from the hospital with no sign of paralysis left in his body." *Star Daily*, "Recovery" The Macalister Par Publishing Co., St. Paul, MN)

Yes there are genuine healings and miracles, but the choice, as always, belongs to the Holy Spirit.

Many volumes of testimonies from the multiplied millions could be added to this testimony validating healings and miracles. To deny this would deny God's infallible Written Word. "Jesus Christ the same yesterday, to day, and forever." (Hebrews 13:8)

"He performs wonders that cannot be fathomed, miracles that cannot be counted." (Job 9:10) (NIV)

By the way, I was very serious about the meeting for all of the desperately ill needing a touch from God. Ladies and gentlemen, the church's phone number is (817) 662-6622. May I hear from all the above-mentioned?

11

LET'S GET BACK TO BASICS

The following comment was given by Leon Stewart to the large audience at the 42nd General Council of the Assemblies of God in August, 1987 in Oklahoma City. Rev. Stewart is the General Superintendent of the Pentecostal Holiness Church, headquarters in Oklahoma City, Oklahoma.

He said to the audience of 16,000 delegates:

"I thank God for the Assemblies of God Church. I praise God for my friendship and fellowship with your leadership and especially Brother Zimmerman and Brother Carlson who have been so kind to my wife Donna and I through the years.

"The Assemblies of God! There is no question that you are the greatest Pentecostal denomination in the world. There is no question you are great because you are the largest Pentecostal body in the world. You are not as big as you should be. You are not as big as you ought to be. You are not as big as you're going to be in the next few years. I think all the rest of us depend on you to lead us in missions, education, publications, evangelism, and Christian education. In so many ways, we look to you for leadership.

"May I plead with you tonight in your 42nd General Council? Would you do something for the rest of us? Primarily would you do it for our Friend and Savior, the Lord Jesus Christ?

"Would you lead us out of modern cheap grace and easy believism? Would you lead us out of material greed and self gratification? Would you lead us out of pseudo-psychology and exalted sensationalism? Would you lead us back to the voice that stills the voice of secular humanism? Would you lead us back to the touch of the nail printed hands that produce real and genuine miracles? Would you lead us back to Him, our true example, and that holy life style that leads us upward and ever upward to where the light lingers even when the sun is set? Would you please lead us back to a genuine appreciation of the Lamb of God, our Lord Jesus Christ? And would you please do that? I plead, do it! God bless you!"

Rev. Stewart's plea is a call back to the basics. There is a lot of religion swirling around in America. But it is not a revival of the redemptive work of our Lord Jesus Christ. In the boom of religion that Jesus spoke of, the earmark is that "For many shall come in my name...and shall deceive many." (Matt. 24:5)

Religiosity in general seems to have little to do with the Christian faith. The religion of the Athenians is a composite of deism, materialism, humanism, and such. As in most religions there is a sprinkling of the Bible, just enough to give it a flavor.

According to Dr. Martin E. Marty in his book *The New Shape of American Religion*, a directive was sent to speakers who appeared on their radio and television programs. They said, "In a very real sense we are selling religion, the good news of the Gospel. Therefore, admonitions and training of Christians on cross bearing, forsaking all else, making sacrifices, and offering themselves in service usually cause the average listener to turn the dial.''

SELLING THE GOSPEL?

They are saying, "You shouldn't preach these sort of things; the people will not listen." However, II Corinthians 2:17 and 5:19 include the cross!

They are saying, "You can't hold an audience around a cross. You can use the language of the cross, but you can't hold an audience who will listen to that thirty minutes a night."

This is a sad commentary. If the purpose is not to preach the Gospel of Christ, then why bother? The Gospel is so desperately needed.

The basics? The preaching of the Gospel of the Lord Jesus Christ. The GOSPEL is the power of God unto Salvation. Paul said in II Corinthians 4:11, "For while we live we are always being given up to death for Jesus' sake, so that the life of Jesus may be manifested in our mortal flesh." (RSV) (Phaneroo)

The word "PHANEROO" is used nine times in II Corinthians.

"PHANEROO" means revelation that comes through preaching. Who is that revelation? Jesus!

The preaching of the Written Word of God is the basic, powerful, ministry of the Church. In I Corinthians 2:2; 1:17 we read, "For I resolved to know nothing while I was with you except Jesus Christ and him crucified...For Christ did not send me to baptize, but to preach the gospel - not with words of human wisdom, lest the cross of Christ be emptied of its power." (NIV)

There are those who think the preaching of the Gospel is not mysterious enough. The Gospel mysterious? Yes! Mystic? No! Paul said this, "...mystery was made known to me by revelation...not made known to the sons of men in other generations as it has now been revealed...by the Spirit." (Eph. 3:3, 5) (RSV)

There are a number of preachers and teachers who call their teaching deep. The truth is, no ministry is deeper than the preaching of the Gospel of Jesus Christ. Some ministries have succeeded in stirring up shallow water into mud, till one cannot see the bottom of the shallow pool.

Lord Balfour in his "Foundations of Beliefs" said, "If the atonement were not too wide for our intellectual comprehension, it would be too narrow for our spiritual necessities."

That is a magnificent phrase. "Some people seem to think that they want something deeper to preach about and something more intellectual to listen to. I contend that the subject of a Christ crucified is a theme for a lifetime, for an eternity. You may think it is not up-to-date preaching; but in reality, it is the only kind of preaching that is up-to- date." - Densdale T. Young

"Therefore, if any one is in Christ, he is a new creation; the old has passed away, behold, the new has come. All this is from God, who through Christ reconciled us to himself and gave us the ministry of reconciliation; that is, in Christ God was reconciling the world to himself, not counting their trespasses against them, and entrusting to us the message of reconciliation. So we are ambassadors for Christ, God making his appeal through us..." (II Cor. 5:17-20) (RSV)

We are commissioned to "go" and proclaim the message of the cross of Jesus Christ. A father was talking to his boy about doing a certain chore around the house. The boy gave a dozen reasons why he could not do what his father was asking. Then his father said, "Son, I am not asking you; now do what I said."

The Lord says in Mark 16:15, "...Go ye into all the world, and preach the gospel to every creature."

"There is a story that comes out of the second World War that will haunt you. It is about a little Jewish boy who was living in a small Polish village. He and the other Jews of the community were rounded up by the Nazi troops and sentenced to death.

"This Jewish boy joined his neighbors in digging a shallow ditch to be their own graves. Then they were lined up against a wall and machine-gunned. Their corpses fell into the shallow grave. Nazis covered the bodies with dirt. But none of the bullets had hit the little boy. His naked body was splattered with the blood of his parents, and after falling into the ditch, he pretended to be dead. The grave was so shallow that the thin covering of dirt did not prevent him from breathing.

"Several hours later when darkness fell, this ten year old boy crawled out of the grave. With blood and dirt caked to his little body, he made his way to the nearest home and begged for help.

"As a Jew, the little boy had been marked for death by the Nazis. A woman opened her door, saw him, screamed, and slammed the door. Dirty, bloody, and shivering, the little boy limped from house to house begging for help. At every house, the same response. People were afraid...for he was marked for death.

"Finally in desperation, he knocked on a door, and just before the lady could tell him to leave, he cried out, 'Don't you recognize me? I am the Jesus you say you love.'

"The lady froze in her tracks for what seemed like an eternity to the little boy. Then with tears streaming down her face, she opened her arms. She picked up the little boy and took him inside to safety." (From a sermon by Gary Coleman, Lincolnway Christian Church, New Lenox, Illinois.)

Basics? Preaching the Gospel to save those who have been marked for death!

We must get back to the Bible and the preaching of the Gospel of Jesus Christ.

12

THE WORD OF KNOWLEDGE

HOW GOD SPEAKS TO US TODAY!

"In the beginning was the Word, and the Word was with God, and the Word was God...And the Word was made flesh, and dwelt among us..." (John 1:1, 14)

The super saint personality has accepted the theory that the Lord speaks directly, and they, in turn, tell other people, they have a RHEMA for them. This is the typical "God told me to tell you."

Many have been led to believe that a "Word of Knowledge" reveals the mind of God to them, supposedly in the form of facts about the personal needs of other people. This devious belief is an endeavor to present the notion that man possesses the gifts.

Speaking about spiritual gifts, Paul said in I Corinthians 12:1, "...I would not have you ignorant." His concern expressed to his brethren, was that he did not want them to misunderstand about the gifts. The twelfth chapter of I Corinthians was written to erase this ignorance. The Scripture makes it evident that the gifts are not for a select minority. "But the manifestation of the Spirit is given to every man to profit withal." (I Cor. 12:7)

William Beck says of this verse, "Now the Spirit shows Himself to each one to make him useful."

Since the Word of God is proclaimed from the lips of man, we faulty humans can honestly misunderstand that one might possess the nine gifts.

"A Word of Knowledge" is not one of the three vocal gifts.

The three vocal gifts are tongues, interpretation of tongues, and prophecy.

The audible voice of a human is not a "Word of Knowledge" or "Rhema."

When the Holy Spirit speaks to a member of the Body of Christ, He speaks to our heart, lifting from our mind the written Word of God, what we have previously learned.

Jesus said in John 14:26, "But the Comforter, which is the Holy Ghost, whom the Father will send in my name, he shall teach you all things, and bring all things to your remembrance, whatsoever I have said unto you."

When the Holy Spirit speaks, it is Rhema. Ephesians 6:17, 18 admonishes us to "...take...the sword of the Spirit, which is the word of God: Praying..."

"The references here to the Word of God is not the whole Bible as such, but to the individual verse from Scripture which the Spirit brings to our remembrance for us in time of need. The requirement is that the mind is to be stored regularly with the Scripture." (Vine)

The following is a copulation of several versions of I Corinthians 12:8: "An expression of Spiritual truth, spoken by the Holy Spirit. This phrase, idea, expression of thought, is FACTS about the Holy Spirit. This spiritual truth is a small portion of the LOGOS (Scriptures), or Holy Bible, or the Total Statement of Truth, that becomes real by 'the sword of the Spirit,' bringing to the remembrance of the child of God, the Scriptures already learned. This small portion of truth (Logos) becomes real to the child of God - therefore, 'A WORD OF KNOWLEDGE.'"

When self-appointed prophets claim, "I have a rhema for you," it is not true. Do not believe it. To affirm their statement they say, "God told me to tell you." Their words are as futile as the readings over "tea leaves."

This "Sword of the Spirit" (in Greek, "ten machairan tou Pneumator no estin ehema Theou) refers to the "individual scripture" which the Holy Spirit brings to our remembrance.

The Bible nowhere states that "a Word of Knowledge" is an utterance from man. The Scripture does not even "hint" that it gives facts concerning a personality!

In the context of verses 3-9 in I Corinthians 12, limits would particularly pertain to the means and origin of the Word of Knowledge being found in the Holy Spirit. These phrases establish that an utterance must originate, find its means, and follow the limits of the Holy Spirit-and nothing else. The Word of Knowledge is birthed and communicated by the Holy Spirit. It is not human insight. It is not subject to the power or direction of man. It cannot be given by man.

"Logos" is one of the most significant terms in the New Testament. Christ is called "Word" or "Logos" in John 1:1. The word "Logos" is used to identify the gift of the Word of Knowledge. "Of knowledge" describes the particular kind of "word" involved. The word is revealed "word" from God.

"Gnosis" means knowledge. Paul used this word twenty-three times in the New Testament. It occurs in all the Pauline writings except two. The source of the knowledge is The Knowledge, God feels is important for the believer to hear.

It is important to know that the phrase a "Word of Knowledge" is found in ONLY ONE PLACE IN THE SCRIPTURES and that is in I Corinthians 12:8.

The scriptural conclusion is that a "Word of Knowledge" is spoken to the heart of man by the Holy Spirit.

It is interesting to note that in I Corinthians 12:8, the following Greek words are excluded:

1. RHEMA: the speaking "words."

2. EPOS: the articulation of a particular word.

3. MUTHOS: teaching as a myth or a fable, or a tale that is told.

4. PHONE: voice or vocalized speech. The vocalizing of words or sounds.

Logos is used in I Corinthians 12:8, "A 'WORD' (Logos) of knowledge." Logos means "collecting." It indicates "those things which are collected in thought and then expressed vocally. "Logos" is used when the idea or concept and expression is always understood. The phrase "Word of Knowledge" indicates a gift which is collected in the mind of God. So it is the Logos or Word (the Mind of God) that has become the written Word of God that is spoken in idea form to our heart - Rhema.

The Rhema comes to us as an idea, lifted out of the written word (Logos), at the precise moment of need. This word is spoken with clearness and precision by the Holy Spirit.

The Word of Knowledge is the real facts about salvation (Acts 26), His grace (Acts 14:3), God (II Cor. 2:17), reconciliation (II Cor. 5:19), truth (II Cor. 6:7), the Gospel truth (Eph. 1:13), and Words of Life (Phil. 2:16).

This "Word of Knowledge" is not secular knowledge about medicine, science, psychology, math, history, the future, the anatomy, botany, and so on. IT IS KNOWLEDGE ABOUT GOD! Spiritual knowledge!

A mechanic knocking himself out over a mechanical problem may claim the Lord gave him the answer. He could be right; the Lord can do what He wants to do. But it is illogical to think this sort of knowledge about a motor is "a Word of Knowledge." The knowledge to fix a car is mechanical knowledge. The manufacturer could give you the very same information out of the manual. Even after obtaining this secular information, the problem would still exist. To correct the mechanical problem, a capable mechanic would be necessary. Knowledge about "things" is not "spiritual" knowledge.

Spiritual counsel spoken by the Holy Spirit is not received with the physical ear. To illustrate: the deaf and dumb individual can receive this gift or spiritual knowledge. They can hear the Rhema (voice of the Holy Spirit) in the same way as a person with good physical hearing.

Just to hear is not a miracle. The significance of the Rhema is what we hear and from whom we hear.

The voices, dreams, and visions we usually hear of are

certainly not "the Word of knowledge." The guidebook to judge the credibility of any word, ministry, vision, or dream is the Written Word of God. To have a dream that foretells an event that comes to pass is not the same as a "Word of Knowledge." No message is equal to the Word of God. Romans 10:17 says, "So then faith cometh by hearing, and hearing by the word of God." This refers to hearing the voice of the Spirit, not the hearing of a preacher.

While on his way to minister to our congregation for Sunday services, the airplane composer-singer Derek Floyd was on encountered some unexpected trouble. A few minutes out of Dallas the stewardess announced the air conditioning was on fire. Derek thought, "Is this the end?" He silently prayed, "Lord, are You through with my ministry here on earth?"

First he became afraid, then he became concerned for the other passengers on the airplane. Immediately the Holy Spirit spoke peace to his heart, and then he was not afraid. This was a rhema spoken to Derek's heart. The Word became knowledge, and the Holy Spirit gave a gift of peace! Only the Holy Spirit could speak this silent phrase to Derek. It was a miracle of hearing, spoken by the Holy Spirit.

The Word of Knowledge is pure, unmixed with man's ideas. The Holy Spirit is the only qualified person to speak, to whom He wills. The Holy Spirit speaks the truth and nothing but the truth.

The knowledge is not "gnosis," which is regarded as a technical term for gnostic heresy (I Tim. 6:20). The definition of gnostic is "possessing mystical knowledge." So a Word of Knowledge is definitely not of a mystical (magic) and technical nature.

The Holy Spirit speaks only actual Christlike knowledge.

The "Gnostics" were a religious sect. They flourished in Western Asia and Egypt between 250 B.C. and 400 A.D. Early Christian literature in the first and second centuries unsparingly condemned gnosticism. But later, it was erroneously recognized that a gnostic might also be a good Christian. The gnostic knowledge was projected of a celestial character that secured the protection of the Great God.

In short, gnosticism received revelations (not scriptures); they used amulets (objects worn to protect them from accidents) and hoped to secure knowledge of a celestial nature and protection for themselves; they considered the Virgin Mary and others equal with Christ.

The first two of the above are practiced today by some charismatic ministries.

Paul refers to real knowledge with the Greek word "Epignosis," which means Christ knowledge. (I Tim. 2:4; 2:25; Titus 1:11) This knowledge is conferred to the believer when one is born again by the Spirit.

Paul spoke of the Jews as having a zeal for God but not "kata epignosis" or real knowledge. This mysterious knowledge belongs only to the saints. "The mystery hidden for ages and generations but now made manifest to his saints." (Col. 1:26) (RSV)

When the Holy Spirit speaks, His judgments are always suitably received. That which characterizes the RHEMA is ONLY the Holy Spirit speaks it and there are always results. In other words, the person in need always understands when the Spirit speaks to him. Otherwise, He would not will to speak. The Holy Spirit does not throw away His words.

As the Holy Spirit inspired holy men to speak the mind of God, scribes wrote the words down on parchment; this "Rhema" became "Logos", (the preserved total statement of God). The cannon is now closed, but Rhema is still spoken to the hearts of believers. The Lord speaks to man today that which was written down in Bible days as holy men spake. The cannon is the sixty-six books of the Bible we hold dear.

Now, in the church age (almost 2,000 years), the Holy Spirit brings to remembrance what we have studied and memorized of the Scriptures.

The present day operation of the nine gifts of the Holy Spirit was not given to the Church until after the day of Pentecost. It is not disrespectful to say that Jesus did not need the nine gifts. The gifts are for the Church.

The following versions of I Corinthians 12:11 express the Holy Spirit's sovereignty: "...severally as he will." (KJV)

and, "Distributing to each individual as He pleases." (ML)

134

and, "It is the same and only Holy Spirit who gives all these gifts and powers, deciding which each one of us should have." (LB)

and, "...who apportions to each one individually as he wills." (RSV)

The Rhema is not handed down or handed out by human instruments. "Revelation takes place" given by the Holy Spirit.

Gifts received by a believer cannot be transferred to another believer. To illustrate: when the Holy Spirit wills to give the sick person the gift of healing, that person cannot prefer someone else to receive the healing. The gift is particular to that person.

Correspondingly when the Spirit speaks "spiritual truth" to a believer, this knowledge cannot be transferred from one human mind to another. No preacher, prophet, apostle, or fortune teller can dole out gifts to others.

Some project the idea that a special few possess one or more of the nine gifts and this elite few supposedly dole out the gifts to others!

It is true that we have an unction (a spiritual fervor) but that unction originates from the Holy Spirit. This anointing is not an art or human ability of man. The axe-head in the Old Testament story is a type of what we have...it is an anointing...but it is borrowed. We only swing the axe-handle. The Holy Spirit is the cutting edge. Just as the axe-head was lost, so we too can lose that special anointing. (See II Kings 6:5)

In the same way, the gifts of the Holy Spirit may be compared to an automobile that belongs to someone else. You may use it, but not sell, give away or abuse it. It does not belong to you. The gifts are exercised by members of His body as we preach, teach, and exhort the Written Word of God. Human agency is involved in "handling the Word of God," but THE GIFTS RESIDE IN THE HOLY SPIRIT, not in man.

At the World's Fair, an exhibition portrayed what appeared to be a man pumping water. At first glance from a distance, it looked like a real man. But as one drew near, it was clear to see that a stream of water was actually moving a mechanical man. The man was not giving power to the pump; the moving water was giving power to the man. So it is with the Holy Spirit, we preach and teach under the anointing.

The exercising of a gift in a regular fashion indicates that the believer has a charisma that provides a basis for an ongoing ministry. According to Paul, all believers may prophesy, (I Cor. 14:5) but some have a continuing ministry of this kind.

I Corinthians 12:6 states, "And there are diversities of operations, but it is the same God which worketh all in all."

Man is never the source of power. At best all we can do is just work the pump handle! To be more precise, we handle the Bible, The Word of God. W. J. Conybeare comments on I Corinthians 12:1, "Now concerning the spiritual gifts, brethren..." and says, "Concerning those who EXERCISE spiritual gifts brethren."

Christians are to be very cautious of gift theology, or the obsession that God throws out His gifts for people to posses like something we carry in our hip pocket. Gift theology (ownership by man) carried to its logical conclusion, so downgrades purposed understanding of the Scriptures, as to make the Bible record match oneself's own interested position.

"The Word of Knowledge," one of the nine gifts, is a post-pentecost gift. The word used for gifts here is the Greek word, "ton pneumalikon" and is defined in I Corinthians 12:7 as "The manifestation of the spirit" that is given to "every man to profit with all." The parent word for this manifestation is "pneumatikos," a word that "Always connotes the ideas of invisibility and of power. It does not occur in the Septuagint, nor the Gospels; it is in fact an after pentecost word."

The Holy Spirit's power is unrelenting in His distribution of the Gifts. Man cannot mishandle nor misdirect the gifts for they do not issue from man, but burst forth from the Spirit of God. He is sovereign in His distribution to believers. (I Cor. 12:4) The individual believer used of the Lord can misbehave in exercising the gifts. But the gifts are distributed only by the Holy Spirit, who is never in error.

Greek scholar J.H. Thayer interprets the gifts as: "The extraordinary powers distinguishing certain Christians and enabling them to serve the Church of Christ, the reception of which is due to the power of divine grace operating in the soul by the Holy Spirit."

It was true in the early church and is the same today that these gifts are the deposit of the Holy Spirit within the members of the body of Christ in particular. We are the earthly temple in which the Holy Spirit dwells.

Unger says of I Corinthians 12:8, "Paul here refers strictly to the "gift of knowledge". By this special gift the Holy Spirit enabled the first century Christians to know and to instruct the assembly in truth, now recorded in the New Testament."

This Word of Knowledge is not facts about people, history, places, or incidents out of the Bible. It is not calling a person to the ministry or to the mission field, etc. It is spiritual truth singled out of the written Word of God by the Spirit and applied to the believer's heart, meeting a spiritual need.

A Word of Knowledge from the Holy Spirit to the believer enables one to grasp a truth about a present situation: seeing, knowing, understanding as the Holy Spirit sees, knows, and understands.

The person at the pump represents one's handling the Word of God. Word handlers must be "approved workmen not to be ashamed." It is not necessary, nor is it beneficial, that the preacher or the teacher knows what the Holy Spirit reveals to other believers. Gifts are personal miracles to the believer's heart.

A Word of Knowledge is not identical to other revelations in the Old and New Testaments and should not be confused with revelations such as:

1. God revealed to Elisha the whereabouts of a Syrian camp and all that went on there. (II Kings 6:11-12)

2. God revealed to Peter that Annanias and his wife were lying. (Acts 5:3-4)

3. Paul knew that the ship was doomed on the way to Rome and there would be no loss of lives. (Acts 5:3-4)

4. When Paul, filled with the Holy Ghost, set his eyes on him and said, "O full of subtlety and all mischief thou child of the Devil...wilt thou cease to pervert the right ways of the Lord?" (Acts 13:9-11)

These supernatural revelations and numerous more could be cited, are not precisely the same as the "manifestation of the Spirit," that is given to every believer as stated in I Corinthians 12:7. Again I state that the Greek word Charismata, for gifts is a post-Pentecost word.

The nine gifts of the Spirit (spirituals) is God's formula for the church age (Pentecost to Rapture) and was established for the day of grace. There are similarities to the Holy Spirit's working in the Old Testament, but it's not the same operation.

Hebrews 1:1, 2 states, "God, who at sundry times and in divers manners spake in time past unto the fathers by the prophets, hath in these last days spoken appointed heir of all things, by whom also he made the worlds."

Since Pentecost, gifts are given to every man whereas the Old Testament revelations and miracles were restricted generally within the prophets' ministry.

It is unreasonable (unintelligent) to suggest that if a believer has not been prophesied over by a charismatic fortune-teller, he has not received a Word of Knowledge. In preference to hearing God through a "Super Spiritual" (so called), the Holy Spirit speaks directly to the believer. (I Cor. 12:7)

The Scriptures admonish us to rightly divide the written Word of God. I Peter 4:11 speaks of how we handle the written Word of God. When we speak, we must speak as the "oracles" of God (logia Theou). This is in reference to speaking the written Word bathed in prayer under the anointing of the Holy Spirit. "If any man speak, let him speak as the oracles of God; if any man minister, let him do it as of the ability which God giveth: that God in all things may be glorified through Jesus Christ, to whom be praise and dominion for ever and ever." (KJV)

The "ability which God giveth" intimates that there is an anointing that enables us as we minister. The words "if any man" include prophet, preacher, and teacher in worship. This is whether instruction in a mission of the community, or as an individual privately encouraging evangelization, or rebuking another Christian or even pagan. Hence the speaker is urged not to give his own opinion or be motivated by self-esteem, but to speak what is given to him as God's Word to the glory of God.

"Knowing this first, that no prophecy of the scripture is of any private interpretation. For the prophecy came not in old time by the will of man: but holy men of God spake as they were moved by the Holy Ghost." (II Peter 1:20, 21) (KJV)

Note: No prophecy of Scripture is of any private inter-pretation (epiluis) or not thought up by the prophet himself. Peter is saying that when we speak, we should be careful not to convey what we think, hope, or imagine. The essence of many prophecies is only the words of man.

Paul warned Timothy about the traveling preachers who had their own version of Apostolic preaching (kerygma) in I Timothy 6:20: "O Timothy, keep that which is committed to thy trust, avoiding profane and vain babblings, (Godless chatter) and oppositions of science falsely so called." (KJV)

Now the same verse in the Living Bible reads this way: "Oh, Timothy, don't fail to do these things that God en-trusted to you. Keep out of foolish arguments with those who boast of *their* "knowledge" and thus prove their lack of it."

The profane babblings and knowledge Paul is speaking of is the secular knowledge that comes out of man, rather than spiritual knowledge out of the written Word of God, made real to us by the Holy Spirit.

"We might listen to Scripture and hear only words, a man's word, which we do not understand. It is then the corre-sponding event is still wanting. What we heard was the writ-ten word, which we receive, was not the Word of God." -Karl Barth

THE WORD OF KNOWLEDGE IS A SPIRITUAL Gift, KNOWLEDGE, ONLY SPOKEN by the Holy Spirit, a small portion of the LOGOS, an idea or phrase uttered by the Holy Spirit, and the written Word of God is made alive and always heard.

THE "WORD OF KNOWLEDGE" IS NOT secular knowledge that is transferable to another person (the attempt to retell "a Word of Knowledge" is not rhema.) "A word of knowledge" is not a physical diagnosis about sickness or symptoms, a reading by one person about another, prophecy, discernment, guessing anything, probability statements, percentage statements, spoken by the believer, psychomancy (divination by reading a personality), Theomancy (divination by using the Scriptures), mind reading/mental telepathy, fortune-telling, palm reading, handed down or handed out, or a lucky guess about people, places, and things.

The Bible came into being when the "rhema" and written Word were the same. The rhema was spoken by the Holy Spirit, heard by holy men of God, then written down - thus becoming "logos," or the sixty-six books of the Bible.

In Acts 13:16-41, Paul preaches a sermon. The "spiritual" was silently spoken to him from the Holy Spirit. It was written down as Paul spoke it to people. When it was written down, it became logos and was later gathered into the cannon. In II Peter 3:2, Peter says, "That ye man be mindful of the words which were spoken [rhema] before by the holy prophets, and of the commandment of us the apostles of the Lord and Saviour." (KJV)

The Living Bible's rendering of this same verse reads, "I have tried to remind you - if you will let me - about facts you already know: facts you learned from the holy prophets and from us apostles who brought you the words of our Lord and Savior."

So the Word of God in Scripture brought to Peter's remembrance, rhema, became logos and entered into the New Testament.

Rhema is used in Romans 10:8, ..."The word [Rhema] is nigh thee, even in thy mouth, and in thy heart: that is, the word of faith, which we preach." (KJV)

Jesus is "the Word" - not "a word" of knowledge!

He was the Word of God, not a psychic or any other unreal occultist. John 3:34 says, "For he whom God hath sent speaketh the words [Rhema] of God: for God giveth not the Spirit by measure unto him." (KJV)

Realistically, when the Holy Spirit reveals to us the Word, Jesus becomes factual or real to us.

Hebrews 4:12 says, "For the word of God is quick, and powerful...and is a discerner of the thoughts and intents of the heart." (KJV)

The Living Bible states the same verse this way: "...cutting swift and deep into our innermost thoughts and desires with all their parts, exposing us for what we really are."

So Jesus (The Word) cuts deep into our thoughts and exposes us for what we are. This is what some modern day prophets claim when they give their alleged "Word of Knowledge."

In James 1:23-24 we read, "Anyone who listens to the word but does not do what it says is like a man who looks at this face in a mirror and after looking at himself, goes away and immediately forgets what he looks like."

The mirror is compared to the written Word of God. As we look into the Bible, the written Word, the SWORD OF THE SPIRIT discerns the person looking into the Word. When we look into the mirror, we do not view the beauty nor the faults of another person. The revelation is only to the person looking into the mirror.

The way the believer hears from God is: 1. To learn and know the Bible. "Study to show thyself approved." 2. To pray for the Holy Spirit to make the Word real to the heart. 3. To walk in the Spirit daily, and the Holy Spirit will bring the Scriptures needed to live a victorious Christian life.

Man is not gifted to discern the spiritual condition of another person. Only the Word of God cuts swift and deep into our innermost thoughts and intents of the heart. This is why it is imperative that believers learn to proclaim the written Word and not our own thoughts. Any person who claims to read another person's mail is claiming nothing short of occultism.

People often say, "That preacher was talking right to me."

They suspected somebody had told the preacher about their sinning. Nothing could be farther from the truth. It is the Word of God that discerns the thoughts and intents of the heart. PREACHING AND TEACHING THE WRITTEN WORD OF GOD under the anointing is what believers are to do.

Some infer that Jesus performed miracles and healings while He was on earth and since He is gone, we do what He did 2,000 years ago. This logic is free-thinking and is irreverent. Jesus only performed genuine healings and miracles, and He still does them today. All believers can do is preach the Gospel, which is the power of God. More preaching, more spreading of the Gospel equals a greater amount of results. History does not record any personality (other than Jesus) stilling a storm, walking on water, and raising the dead after "they stinketh." That has happened but it was the power of Jesus, not man's power!

MAN IS INCAPABLE OF PERFORMING MIRACLES AND HEALINGS! Jesus is the "WORD" that produces true unimaginary results. "For he spake, and it was done; he commanded, and it stood fast." (Psalm 33:9) (KJV)

Jesus told His disciples (not as a clairvoyant) that they would, "...enter the city, a man carrying a jar of water will meet you...He will show you a large upper room, all furnished." (Luke 22:10-12) (NIV)

Jesus, the Word, knew these facts, not through occultic power, but because He was God. Occult activity is a lean counterfeit, not a replica of the Word of Knowledge. The occult is a secret, unknowable power. It is not co-equal or the same brand as spiritual knowledge. Occult power is suggestions that allude to information about a person's health, wealth, happiness, and so on. That which saturates most charismatic fortune-telling is unclear prognostication. If that were the same as a Word of Knowledge, it would not be counterfeit. The source and purpose of spiritual knowledge is miles apart from occultism. The Word of Knowledge is not cloudy facts about people; it is knowledge about Jesus Christ from the Holy Spirit!

Jesus' omniscient knowledge was so, that people asked, "What is this which is given unto Him?"

Men of learning said, "How knoweth this man letters,

having never learned?''

No "man's" learning resembles this level of knowledge.

Jesus did not serve in the limited realm as a pastor or evangelist. John 4:39 says, "Many Samaritans from that city believed in him because of the woman's testimony, 'He told me all that I ever did.' '' (RSV)

Jesus' knowledge as the Word here was unmistakably accurate. Occult powers can impart pieces of factual information. Only Jesus, the Word, is 100-25- accurate. He did not depend on percentages and probability factors.

Because Jesus was THE WORD, He knew Nathanael by name. In John 1:48, Nathanael asked, "How do you know me?" Jesus answered, "I saw you while you were still under the fig tree before Philip called you." (NIV)

THE OLD REGULATOR

A man entered the store of a jeweler who had purchased a shipment of clocks. They were many sizes and kinds. All the clocks had been wound and started at different times. No two told the same tale. While one was striking twelve, another was striking three. To say the least, all these clocks having a different time created confusion. The visitor watching all of these clocks was laughing at the situation. He said, "If by accident one of the clocks told the correct time, we still could not be for sure."

But the merchant pointed to an old "REGULATOR" hanging in the corner of the room. The tick was deliberate and steady. The owner said, "There is the correct time. None of these other clocks have been regulated or set. But that Old Regulator in the corner is checked up every hour, government time."

WHAT IS THE REGULATOR OF LIFE? The Bible! Men, organizations, doctrines, practices, and such are represented by the other little clocks. But every person and teaching is "false" unless in harmony with the Old Regulator, the written Word of God!

Man often finds himself confused over the different interpretations and expressions of religious truth. With seemingly everyone claiming to be the divinely appointed teachers of the truth, we should wisely check everything with the Bible!

Remember some timepieces, are too fast, some too slow, the hands are beautiful, the face is attractive, BUT THERE IS SOMETHING WRONG WITH THE WORKS!